ETHNIC IDENTITIES AND DEMOCRACY

Electrol Politics in North East India

Apurba K. Baruah
Rajesh Dev

2025

Regency Publications
A Division of
Astral International Pvt. Ltd.
New Delhi – 110 002

First Published, 2006

Reprinted, 2025

ISBN: 978-81-89233-41-9

Disclaimer:

Every possible effort has been made to ensure that the information contained in this book is accurate at the time of going to press, and the publisher and author cannot accept responsibility for any errors or omissions, however caused. No responsibility for loss or damage occasioned to any person acting, or refraining from action, as a result of the material in this publication can be accepted by the editor, the publisher or the author. The Publisher is not associated with any product or vendor mentioned in the book. The contents of this work are intended to further general scientific research, understanding and discussion only. Readers should consult with a specialist where appropriate.

Every effort has been made to trace the owners of copyright material used in this book, if any. The author and the publisher will be grateful for any omission brought to their notice for acknowledgment in the future editions of the book.

Published by : **Regency Publications**
A Division of
Astral International Pvt. Ltd.
– ISO 9001:2015 Certified Company –
4736/23, Ansari Road, Darya Ganj
New Delhi-110 002
Ph. 011A43549197, 23278134
E-mail: info@astralint.com
Website: www.astralint.com

Printed at : **Replika Press Pvt. Ltd.**

Acknowledgements

We as editors would like to express our appreciation to the contributors who made this volume possible. We would also like to place on record our appreciation for the *Lokniti* programme of the Centre for the Study of Developing Societies (CSDS), New Delhi because as founder members of that programme we learnt to look at electoral politics from a perspective that makes the study of elections more meaningful. The editors are particularly grateful to V.B. Singh and Yogendra Yadav for the instructive interactions about election studies in the early phase of the *Lokniti* programme. The programme has been able to generate considerable amount of data as part of our collective effort during the numerous election studies since 1996. Our obligation to members of the North Eastern Institute of Development Studies (NEIDS), particularly Manorama Sharma & Patricia Mukhim, for supporting this venture in numerous ways must be publicly recorded. We have freely used the archive of paper clippings maintained in NEIDS for these papers for which we are indebted to Aitilyn Blah and Naba Kumar Mahanta. Our sincere thanks are due to all those friends who improved the contents of this volume through their critical comments. Finally, we thank Mr. Arun Verma of Regency Publications who undertook this task of publishing this volume despite a demanding schedule.

Shillong
November 2005

Apurba K. Baruah
Rajesh Dev
(Editors)

Contents

List of Contributors

Apurba K. Baruah is a Professor of Political Science at North Eastern Hill University (NEHU), Shillong. His major works include *Systems Analysis in Political Science* (New Delhi, 1987), *Social Tensions in Assam: Middle Class Politics* (Guwahati, 1991), *Student Power in North East India* (New Delhi, 2002). He has completed a major project on *Community, Conflicts and Crisis of Governance: An Analysis of the Societies of North East India*, as a part of the Crisis States Programme of London School of Economics and Political Science and published a number of working papers in www.crisisstates.com. Baruah is one of the General Editors of *North East India Studies*.

Rajesh Dev teaches Political Science at Women's College, Shillong and was a guest lecturer to the Department of Law, North Eastern Hill University, Shillong. He had been a UGC Senior Research Fellow at NEHU for his doctoral research. Besides being a contributor of essays to edited volumes and journals like the *Economic & Political Weekly*, he is one of the Editors of *Ethnonarratives: Identity & Experience in Northeast India*. Dev contributes to regional and national dailies and has been a Resource Person for IGNOU and the NCERT. He is currently the State Co-ordinator for Meghalaya of the Centre for the Study of Developing Societies' *Lokniti* Programme. He was associated with the Crisis States Programme of the London School of Economics and Political Science.

Pascal Malngniang is a Reader of Political Science at North Eastern Hill University Shillong. His major works include *Students & Politics in Meghalaya* (Shillong, 1994).

Bhagat Oinam is an Associate Professor of Philosophy at Jawaharlal Nehru University, New Delhi. His major works have been in the areas of Moral Philosophy and Identity

Politics. Oinam has been publishing in major research journals and news papers of the country.

Manas Paul is a senior Journalist based in Tripura. He has been reporting on Tripura for the regional and the national press.

Abbreviations

1. INC	Indian National Congress
2. BJP	Bharatiya Janata Party
3. SAP	Samata Party
4. DPP	Democratic Peoples' Party
5. MSCP	Manipur State Congress Party
6. MPP	Manipur Peoples Party
7. MNC	Manipur National Conference
8. FPM	Federal Party of Manipur
9. JD (U)	Janata Dal (United)
10. JD (S)	Janata Dal (Secular)
11. CPI	Communist Party of India
12. NNP	Naga National Party
13. KNA	Kuki National Assembly
14. IND	Independent
15. AC	Assembly Constituency
16. DAN	Democratic Alliance of Nagaland

Electoral Politics as a Field of Study in North East India: Some Introductory Remarks

In any country practising a form of representative democracy study of electoral politics should be of considerable importance because it is the èlectoral process that sustains the democratic governance. In most of the democratic countries electoral politics has become a major field of study. Interest in the study of elections in the western democracies can be traced back even to the nineteenth century. Teer and Spence had shown that by the end of the nineteenth century *Columbus Despatch* was doing stratified interviews.[1] Voter turn out was studied and published in America as early as 1920s.[2] The successful predictions or forecasts made by Gallup poll, Crossly poll and fortune survey in the 1936 presidential election increased interest in election surveys in the United States. In United Kingdom too Gallup poll began predicting results on the basis of surveys from 1938 itself. Such predictions interested not only political parties and candidates but also *inter alia* created enormous interest among serious scholars of politics because predictions helped in identifying trends. The fortunes of the pollsters fluctuated regularly but the surveys done for the purpose of forecast definitely prompted serious scholars to take to election studies. By the early twentieth century a large number of scholars in the west began emphasising the role of voters in determining the health of democracy and a new methodology of electoral studies with a particular ideological underpinning seemed to emerge. It indeed is true that almost all those scholars who participated in this exercise during the period of its emergence as a special field considered only the western liberal democracy as democracy. Defining dêmocracy as a system of representative governance ensuring individual freedom and availability of political choices, they came to look only at multiparty systems of governance as democratic. In this perspective the liberal aspects of democratic governance was grounded more in a formal availability of choices and the possibilities of exercising freedom of choice in the negative sense than the egalitarian dimensions of political participation. Ideologues and scholars of this school maintain that in constitutional democracies elections act as the means of determining who will govern and for what purposes. In this perception the concept of representation of popular will is tied to the idea of free elections and political representation is taken to be implicit in the very idea of constitutional governance. Social scientists like V.O. Key, Angus Campbell or Philip E. Converse[3] who pursued electoral research broadly from behavioural perspectives would not have accepted C.B. Macpherson's assertion in *The Real World of Democracy*, that in the modern world we have three different kinds of democracies rooted in three different realities and systems of values[4] and would have upheld what he called an old die hard habit of thought, "[M]ost of the backward countries were in colonial tutelage of liberal-democratic states, and...before being granted independence they were to be brought along to the point where they would run themselves on liberal-democratic lines."[5] These scholars focused mainly on elections in societies with multiparty systems that introduced universal adult suffrage.

Indian political science originally being an offshoot of the western version of the discipline followed the methodological tools and systems of analysis used by their western peers. We have shown elsewhere that mainstream Political Science in India has been using the concepts popularised by the western Political Science without realising that concepts are not neutral.[6] It was therefore natural for the election studies in India to adopt the methodology followed in the west. It was with such a methodology that these studies began in India after the first general elections of independent India. Some Political Scientists did notice certain problems in this methodology. An evaluation of the election studies in India had rightly concluded that if we looked at the studies of Indian elections in the fifties, we would find them rather simplistic, descriptive and generic type.[7] But some notable efforts were made at producing fruitful studies of Indian elections by Gogekarand

Park,[8] D.P. Mukherjee[9] and W.H. Morris Jones.[10] Studies on Indian elections acquired considerable importance in the fifties and researches at doctoral levels were carried out. Of these early efforts one of the most important was E.R. O'Connor's 'India and Democracy: An analysis of the 1951–52 Elections and Their Political Impact', submitted to the University of Notre Dame in 1954. All these studies of course were influenced by the pioneering work done in the field in the United States of America in the preceding decades. Guided by the basic behavioural approach to the studies of elections, these studies focused on "value neutral" analysis of electoral hard data and in the process left out the major ideological implications of electoral politics in the new republic. Regional perspective was totally absent because the focus was on the functioning of democracy in the state of India, viewed as a nation state. The behavioural methodology robbed those studies of any socio-economic and ideological analysis of electoral politics also. This trend seemed to continue till the sixties of the last century. Books like G.L. Srivastava's *Indian Elections and Election Petitions*[11] tried to bring in the legal perspective but methodologically remained firmly with the western, particularly American perspective, of electoral analysis. With writings of Rajni Kothari, V.M. Sirsikar and Iqbal Narain in the sixties studies on electoral politics of India began using sophisticated methodology of voting behaviour studies and a lot of empirical data was generated.[12] The trend seemed to continue till seventies.[13] By 1969 the Centre For the Study of Developing Societies (CSDS) began a programme on the party system and electoral behaviour in India and under this programme Ramashray Roy carried out a major work that focused on the democratic consciousness.[14] It is only with interventions of a group of scholars under the programmes sponsored by the Indian Council of Social Science Research and the Centres like the CSDS that a new generation electoral analysis began that tried to break out of the American Voting behaviour fold and began analysing Indian electoral behaviour in the historical and socio-economic context of the country.

All those studies focussed more on who voted how and why? And thus analysis of voting behaviour on caste lines became one of the major trends. This line of analysis threw considerable light on certain social aspects of electoral politics and eventually led to analysis of support structures of parties from caste and at times class perspectives. But these studies took it for granted that it was natural for people to vote. Many lamented at the low rate of polling in elections without inquiring in to the question whether voting mattered for the large sections of the electorate. Do elections offer real political choices to the electorate? By voting a particular party from among the ones contesting Indian elections can the Indian voter change his or her own lot? Such questions were beyond those studies. We had tried to raise some of these issues in the context of the general elections held up to 1978. With the help of analysis of the political goals of the major contesting parties we showed that because of lack of alternative political choice Indian voters of that period were not interested in voting.[15] However, the generation of empirical data continued mainly on the basis of survey work and compilation of the official data. Psephologists like V.B. Singh, David Butler and Pronoy Roy contributed considerably in this direction.

By 1996 a major initiative in electoral analysis was initiated by a group of social scientists that came together under a CSDS programme called *Lokniti.* This group began conducting massive surveys and analysis of survey and aggregate data from socio-economic perspectives. With this initiative psephology seems to have taken off in India. From India's northeast a group comprising Apurba K. Baruah, as the co-ordinator, Sandhya Goswami, K. Debbarma, Pascal Malngiang and Rajesh Dev actively participated in the *Lokniti* surveys. Some members of this group published major papers on the basis of the surveys.[16] Because of publication of the data generated by these surveys in National dailies like *The Hindu* and *The Times of India* and the research outputs of this group in internationally circulated magazines like the *Economic and Political Weekly, Frontline* and *India Today* election studies on North East India received unprecedented visibility. But the history of election studies in Northeast began long before this effort.

Amalendu Guha set a trend in his project on electoral politics. The book that came out of this project became famous more as a book on history of Assam than on electoral politics.[17] Based on official records, aggregate data, and records of non-governmental sources from a historical perspective Guha did a commendable job of analysing the electoral politics of the period covered. In the eighties two titles on electoral politics of the region was published.

K.M. Deka *et al.*, *Election Politics in Assam*[18] tried to study the voting behaviour in Dibrugarh district of Assam in the sixth general election to the Assam Assembly. This volume was the result of an ICSSR sponsored project carried out by a group of political scientists from Dibrugarh University. The project followed the established voting behaviour methodology. In a preface the authors state, "The present work based on a study of the sixth general election to the Assam Legislative Assembly is an analysis of electoral politics and voting behaviour in Assam."[19] Sadly, this effort did not show any awareness of the methodological debates and perspectives that prevailed in the discipline at the time. The book had no section on review of the existing literature on the theme; the literature cited in various chapters did not show any awareness of the theories of voting behaviour or electoral studies in India or any other countries of the world. Despite a section on perspective, the blissful unawareness about the theoretical and ideological issues involved in electoral and voting behaviour studies forced this effort to remain more or less empiricist in nature, devoid of any theoretical conclusions. The chapter on perspectives included in the book merely informs the readers of the socio-economic facts as found in official documents and provides some information on "[T]hree major developments (that) marked the political process in the state during March 1972 to February 1977."[20] In the part II of the book there is a section on methodology that gives information about the constituencies chosen and the size of the sample. Though the sample was claimed to be purposive in nature the method of drawing the sample does not show methodological sophistication required for a scientific survey. A look at how the sample was drawn in one of the constituencies will show the technical inadequacy of the method followed. The authors stated, "[I]n Dibrugarh constituency, Dibrugarh municipality had the highest concentration of urban voters (i.e. 42,946 in total). Among the 23 municipal wards *Barbari* ward was selected for random sampling because it was the most populous ward with 4,242 voters."[21] There was no explanation as to how actually a sample of 200 respondents was drawn from among the 4,242. More importantly the researchers did not find it necessary to consider whether being merely "most populous ward" had helped them to draw a really representative sample. The scholars did not seem to realise that each constituency has small but important subgroups and it was necessary to use a booster method to reflect the responses of such groups.[22]

S.K. Chaube's *Electoral Politics in North East India,* based on another ICSSR sponsored project, presents a far more comprehensive account of the electoral politics of the region because it throws light on the general electoral politics in the context of sixth Lok Sabha election. This book makes a much better use of the aggregate data available in official sources and uses methodology of political history rigorously to produce a useful narrative. So far as the methods and research objectives are concerned this cannot be called a book on electoral politics. The attempt is "...to record the developments up to the seventh Lok Sabha elections in northeast India, the volume tries to describe, and analyse, the on going process of politics in Northeast India, the sixth Lok Sabha elections (1977) forming its core."[23] It is thus clear that the studies of this genre did not really help us understand the electoral politics of the region, though they remain valuable sources of information.

The papers in the present volume provide us with analyses of the electoral politics of almost all states of the northeastern region of India, barring Arunachal Pradesh and Mizoram. The main focus of this volume is on the influence and impact of ethnic plurality of the region upon electoral politics and its consequences for liberal democratic governance. Though the papers differ in their approaches and foci on the issues confronting the respective states, they are knitted together by their concern for ethnic fractures and its political value in a largely ethnically polarised region. In other parts of India caste has been playing a significant role in determining the electoral fortunes of Parties. In the 1990s elections in Bihar, Uttar Pradesh, Haryana and other parts of the country have been found to be influenced by caste.[24]

Like caste in other parts of India, ethnicity and ethnic cleavages play an influential role in determining electoral outcomes in all the states of the region. As such in the paper on elections in Assam, Baruah while outlining the ethnic divisions in the state and the relative influence of each of the ethnic groups in their areas of dominance, points out that the rise of the dominant *Asomiya* nationalism inspired the rise of formidable regional fronts like the Asom Gana Parishad (AGP). In fact the AGP is a reflection of the consolidation of the increasingly assertive regional bourgeoisie that sought to capture political power from national political parties like the Congress who managed to influence a major section of the *Asomiya* Middle Class from the beginning of the twentieth century.[25] The initial success of the AGP had a 'demonstration effect' on the influential sections of other smaller ethnic groups and parties like the Autonomous State Demand Committee (ASDC) represented their voice in Assam and also encouraged already existing regional forces in the hill areas of the region. Nonetheless, till the emergence of formidable regional parties like the AGP, the Congress had the mandate of the *Asomiya* educated middle-class. But after the 1985 ascendancy of the AGP mainly because of its support from those inspired by the anti-foreigners movement, the Congress seems to have lost much of its traditional base to the AGP and later also to the Natun Asom Gana Parishad (NAGP), a splinter group of AGP.

The paper clearly exhibits the fact that since 1977 the Congress has performed better in non-Asomiya dominated areas, given its "national" orientations, the non-Assamese people saw it as a safety valve in the face of the emergence of the regionally inclined *Asomiya* bourgeois represented by the AGP. But Assam Congress' near total dependence on the central leadership, which failed to appreciate the aspirations of the Assamese Middle Class in the area of protection of *Asomiya* identity and also the concern of this class about being neglect of the developmental activity, as Baruah shows has contributed enormously to the decline of the Congress in Assam. The paper highlights the emerging plurality in Assam and its impact on electoral outcomes and therefore, identifies "ethnic identity" as a crucial issue in all post-1970 electoral outcomes. Finally, the paper discusses the "shifting loyalties" in Assam Politics and their impact on the support base of all major political parties. Baruah's significant conclusion is that Assam, being a multi-ethnic and poly-cultural society, exhibits a different brand of "regionalism" that is articulated not in reference to a single-dominant community only but a coalition of different ethnic forces negotiating their own areas of influence in the electoral arena.

The paper on Meghalaya by Baruah and Malngniang though concentrates upon the elections of 2003, provides a historical background to electoral politics in Meghalaya. The paper in seeking to identify the major "social forces" maintains that in the absence of ideological mobilisations electoral politics are centred on tribe affiliations and thus "kinship loyalties" override political considerations. This paper while subtly acknowledging the emergence of class divisions within the major tribal groups of the state emphasises that it plays no role in polarising electoral outcomes. Explaining how democratic mobilisations in the state synthesises traditional and popular myths of origin to influence electoral outcomes it also shows how assertions by dominant tribal groups alienate 'other' tribal groups and in the process consolidate ethnocentric forces of all groups. A significant assertion made by the authors is that the political class in the state at times rises above ethnic loyalty but only to serve personal interests rather than pursuing ideological or wider political goals.

The third paper by Dev analyses the politics of the elections of 2003 in the state of Nagaland and conceptualises it in terms of the political history of the state. Like the other states in the region even in Nagaland tribal affiliations rather than ideological orientations influence electoral outcomes. However, unlike other states in this state democratic political forces seeking mandate through constitutional processes are often influenced and overshadowed by the "ideologically constituted...non-state actors" of extra-constitutional origin that effectively determine electoral outcomes. This has led to the emergence of a "legitimation dilemma" in the Naga society and substantially influences the legal state structures. Another assessment of this paper is that "inter-tribal conflict and cohesion have a substantial bearing...on the trends and outcomes of electoral politics in the state".

An analysis of the elections in Tripura made by Dev and Paul also emphasises the ethnic plurality in the state and the consequent electoral divisions along ethnic polarisation. The paper highlights the emergence of ethnic insurgency and its impact upon electoral outcomes. Moreover, the paper shows that though there are numerous political parties, operating in the state, the electoral fortunes have been historically shared by the Communist Party of India (Marxist) and the Congress. This paper like the others concludes that ethnicity and ethnic loyalty are the prime electoral and political capital for groups who share tenuous social and political relationships.

The paper by Bhagat on Manipur also reflects the fact that political campaigning and electoral results follow the ethnic pattern and are consolidated around ethnic loyalties of the Nagas and the Meiteis — the two major ethnic groups in the state. This paper reveals the influential role of the insurgents in electoral outcomes and how every political party simultaneously seeks to please "the civil society and the insurgent groups". This paper while analysing the election of 2000 highlights the role of the ethnic groupings and the 'extra-legal' actors and at the same time asserts that the election results are but a reflection of the failure of the ruling power in the state to deliver the basic social and political goods to the people. Inspite of the fact that all the papers highlight the important role played by ethnic identities in electoral politics, the volume does not ignore the role of interests articulated by the politically dominant sections within each ethnic identity. The discussion is informed of the fact that ethnic identity and its politics is not undifferentiated in socio-economic terms.

NOTES AND REFERENCES

1. F. Teer and J.D. Spence, *Political Opinion Polls*, Hutchinson, London, 1973.
2. See for instance, C.E. Merriam and H.F. Gosnell, *Non-voting: Cuuses and Methods of Control*, University of Chicago, Chicago, 1924.
3. For a sample see, E. Burdick and A. Brodbeck (Eds.), *American Voting Behaviour*, Free Press, Glencoe, 1959; P.F. Lazersfeld, B. Berelson and H. Gaudet, *The People's Choice: How the Voter Makes up his Mind in a Presidential Campaign*, Columbia University, New York, 1944. For some latter studies see, P. Williams, 'Electoral Studies and the 1980 Elections in the United States', *Electoral Studies*, 1, pp. 347–354.
4. C.B. Macpherson, *The Real World of Democracy*, Oxford University Press, New York, 1972.
5. *Ibid.*, p. 2.
6. A.K. Baruah, "Mainstream Political Science And Its Pit Falls" *Proceedings of the North East India Political Science Association*, Second Annual Conference, Guwahati, 1992, pp. 44–53.
7. Iqbal Narain, K.C. Pandey, Mohanlal Sharma, (Mrs.) Hansa Rajpal, *Election Studies in India: An Evaluation*, Allied, New Delhi, 1978, pp. 13–14. Most of the information used in this part of the discussion are taken from the seminal work.
8. S.V. Gogekar and Richard Park (ed.), *Report on the Indian General Elections: 1951–52*, Popular Book Depot, Bombay, 1956.
9. D.P. Mukherjee, "First Fruits of General Elections", *Economic Weekly*, Jan. 26, 1952, pp. 65–66.
10. W.H. Moriss Jones, "The Indian Elections" *Economic and Political Weekly*, June 28 and July 5, respectively, pp. 655–56 and 688–91.
11. G.L. Srivastava, *Indian Elections and Election Petitions*, Eastern Book Company, Lucknow, 1961.

12. See, for instance, Iqbal Narain, "Political Behaviour in Rural India: The case of Panchayat Elections in Rajsthan", *Journal of Commonwealth Studies*, July, 1967, pp. 109–129; V.M. Sirsikar, "The Study of Voting Behaviour in India: Limitations and Problems" *Political Science Review*, May, 1962, pp. 54–59; Rajni Kothari "The Take Off Election", *Economic Weekly*, July 1962, pp. 1095–96.
13. See, as an example Aloo Dastur *et al.*, *Voting Pattern in Bombay*, Bombay University, Bombay, 1967; S.P. Verma *et al.*, *Voting Behaviour in a Changing Society: A Case Study of the Fourth General Elections in Rajasthan*, National, Delhi, 1973.
14. Ramashray Roy, *The Uncertain Verdict: A Study of the 1969 Elections on Four Indian States*, Orient Longman, Delhi, 1972.
15. A.K. Baruah and Pramod Kumar, "Why Do Voters Not Vote?" *Economic and Political Weekly*, Vol. Nos. 51–52, pp. 2025–2026.
16. See for example, A.K. Baruah and Sandhya Goswami, "Fractured Identities: Politics in a Multi-Ethnic State", *Economic and Political Weekly*. August 21–28, 1999, pp. 2492–2501; Rajesh Dev, "General Elections 1996, 1998: Community Loyalties and Regional Outlook", *ibid.*, pp. 2481–2485.
17. Amalendu Guha, *Planter Raj to Swaraj*, Indian Council of Historical Research, New Delhi, 1977.
18. K.M. Deka, *et al.*, *Election Politics in Assam*, Bani Prakashan, Guwahati, 1987.
19. *Ibid.*, Preface.
20. *Ibid.*, pp. 1–19.
21. *Ibid.*, p. 141.
22. For an example of successful use of this method see, A. Campbell, G. Gurin and W.E. Miller, *The Voter Decides*, Row Peterson, Evanston, 1954.
23. S.K. Chaube, *Electoral Politics In North East India*, Sangam Books, London, 1985, p. vii.
24. For details see, Francine Frankel *et al.*, *Transforming India*, Oxford University Press, New Delhi, 2000.
25. For a discussion of emergence of the Assamese Middle Class and its ascendance to hegemony see, Manorama Sharma *Social & Economic Change in Assam: Middle Class Hegemony*. Ajanta Publications, N. Delhi, 1990.

End of One Party Dominance: Electoral Politics in Poly-Ethnic Assam*

Apurba K. Baruah

Electoral politics in Assam cannot be understood without taking in to account the history of the composite state of Assam. This state as it was, at the time of beginning of the real electoral politics, with the Assembly elections of 1937, was a state created by the British Government to suit the interests of the colonial powers. It is fairly well known that the present state of Assam includes territories inhabited by a large number of ethnic groups/ communities who migrated to the area at various points of time. These groups are descendants of people of distinct origins with clearly distinguishable cultural markers. Historians make a clear distinction between Assam proper, meaning the Barahmaputra plains and the rest of the areas. The valley has been inhabited by a linguistic community called the *Asomiya*. Ever since the advent of the British in 1826, the colonial power followed a policy of expansion. Through the Yandaboo treaty it initially legitimised its occupation of the territory of the *Ahom* kingdom. It was this territory that was called *Asom* at the time of coming of the British to the area. But over a period of five decades the British expanded their rule, created a composite state of Assam covering almost the entire North-Eastern region of the present-day India. Only the

* Parts of the data presented in this paper appeared in A.K. Baruah and Sandhya Goswami, "Fractured Identities: Politics in a Multi-Ethnic State", *Economic and Political Weekly* in, Aug 21–28, 1999, pp. 2492–2501. The argument now presented has been substantially changed in view of new findings and recent political developments that forced the present author to draw somewhat different conclusions.

Kingdoms of Manipur and Tripura and also the area called the North-East Frontier Area (present Arunachal) were kept out of this composite state.[1] It was in this British created state of Assam the *Asomiya* community came to occupy a hegemonic position, initially under the leadership of the newly emerging educated elite that eventually matured in to a middle class.[2] By the time Assam became fully integrated, in the political sense, to the India this class became the most formidable political force in the region. And therefore in the early years of electoral politics of the state the Congress Party mobilized the support of this class by articulating some of its interest. Like at the "national"[3] level, Congress dominated the electoral politics of the late British and the early post-British period. Till 1996 the party had suffered defeat only in 1978 and 1985 assembly elections (Tables 1, 2 and 3). Even in 1977, when in the rest of India, the Congress Party led by Indira Gandhi was virtually wiped out for the atrocities committed during the Emergency, the electorate in Assam gave the party 10 out of 14 seats in the parliament with 50.6 percent vote share. Its share of votes in the parliamentary elections, up to that period, remained above 45 percent and in the assembly elections; its lowest vote share during this period was 43.5 percent (Table 1). Its debacle in the 1996 elections[4] seemed to have set a new trend reducing it to a much weaker position, but the process of weakening could be traced back to 1970s.

Table 1: Assam Lok Sabha Election Results (1952–85)

Year	Total Seats	Turn out	INC		PSP KMPP (1952)		CPI		Party	Seats	Vote
			Seats	Vote	Seats	Vote	Seats	Vote			
1952	12	47.7	11	45.7	–	10.0	–	–	SOC	1	19.2
1957	12	46.6	9	51.7	2	20.0	–	10.2	INC	1	18.1
1962	12	52.8	9	45.2	2	19.2	–	7.0	AHL	1	3.8
1967	14	59.3	10	45.8	2	12.8	1	8.3	AHL	1	3.8
1971	14	50.7	13	57.0	–	4.6	–	5.7	AHL	1	3.0
1977	14	54.9	10	50.6	–	–	–	1.4	JNP	3	3.58
1980	14*	53.4	2	51.0	–	–	–	–	CPI(M)	–	9.2
1984	14	79.7	4	23.6	–	–	–	1.4	AGP	7	33.4

Note: Remaining seats and votes have gone to either other minor parties or independents.

* Election was held only for two Lok Sabha seats in 1980.

The first major setback for Congress came in the assembly 1978 elections (Table 2), in which it won only eight seats in an assembly of 126 and polled 23.7 percent of the valid votes. But those elections were held after the Janata Party's ascent to power at the centre and the change of government in the centre, leading to corresponding changes in the political alignment in the state, appeared to have affected the results of the elections. Though the same issue of Emergency excesses remained central to the campaigns of both the 1977 parliamentary and 1978 assembly elections yet the results were very different. In 1977 as shown above Congress appeared invincible but in 1978 it appeared vanquished. The forces opposed to Congress except the left aligned with the All Assam Students' Union led movement on foreigners issue during 1978 to 85 and shook Congress' mass base. The movement gave birth to the *Asomiya* regional party the Asom Gana Parishad. In the assembly elections of 1985, the Asom Gana Parishad (AGP) rode on a wave to power, as a result of the now famous 'Assam Movement' on the foreigners' issue, with 63 seats in a house of 126 and polled 34.54 percent votes. The Congress, as the most formidable opponent of the movement, won 25 seats and polled only 23.47 percent votes. Any attempts at understanding the results of that election must take the fact in to account that while the votes of the supporters of the movement remained solidly behind the AGP, the votes of the forces inimical to the movement were divided. The United Minority Front (UMF) captured 17 seats and collected 10.85 percent votes. The left parties put up a remarkable performance during the post-Emergency Assembly election of 1978 with the CPI (M) winning 11 seats and the CPI five seats. The Revolutionary Communist Party of India (RCPI) too won four seats in that election. But in 1985, primarily because of their anti-Assam movement stand, they were almost wiped out. The CPI could not win any seat and the CPI (M) won only two. The Plains Tribal Council of Assam (PTCA) won three seats in Bodo areas and United Tribal Liberation Front (UTNLF), another tribal party, won a single seat. The Congress (S) won four seats. Electoral politics wise 1985 became a turning point in Assam politics. Electoral politics wise the *Asomiya* national regionalism arrived. The weakening of the Congress coincided with the emergence of community based smaller parties often called the regional parties. The one-party dominant system was giving way to a multi-party system in which

Table 2: Assam Vidhan Sabha Election Results (1952–85)

Year	Total Seats	Turn out	INC		CPI		AHL		Party	Seats	Vote	Party	Seats	Vote
			Seats	Vote	Seats	Vote	Seats	Vote						
1952	108	61.1	75	43.5	1	2.8	–	–	SOC	4	13.3	GNC	3	0.6
1957	108	58.6	71	52.4	4	8.1	–	–	PSP	8	12.7	–	–	–
1962	105	52.8	79	48.3	–	6.4	11	5.5	PSP	6	12.7	RCP	1	1.2
1967	126	61.3	73	43.6	7	5.2	9	3.5	PSP	5	6.9	SSP	4	3.3
1972	114	61.7	94	53.2	3	5.6	–	–	SOC	4	5.8	PTC	1	1.7
1978	126	66.9	8	8.8	5	4.1	–	–	INCU	26	23.6	JNP	53	27.6
1983	126	32.7	91	52.5	1	2.1	–	–	PTC	3	4.7	ICS	2	6.1
1985	126	79.2	25	23.2	–	1.2	–	–	AGP	65	35.0	UMF	18	11.8

Note: Remaining seats and votes have gone to either minor parties or independents.

political parties of various ethnic groups or smaller cultural communities began to play significant roles. The support base of the Congress Party showed a steady decline while regional parties based either on regional issues or ethnic aspirations of smaller communities were able to consolidate their hold in Assam politics. Religious and linguistic minorities were also making their presence felt through parties formed specifically to represent their interests. The left parties were very critical of regional, and particularly *Asomiya* regional politics, at least during the turbulent days of the Assam Agitation. But now they appeared to tacitly accept the reality of the regional forces. The period also showed the emergence of Bharatiya Janata Party, which till then had hardly any base in Assam politics, as an important electoral force. Electoral politics in Assam was gradually reflecting the political significance of its multi-ethnic reality, with the respective educated elites of various communities consolidating their hold over the politics of their own communities.

Rise of *Asomiya* Nationalism and Electoral Performances

In the 1991 assembly elections the Congress staged a remarkable comeback by winning 65 seats and polling 29 percent votes; but this did not actually reflect a resurgence of support for Congress. A quick look at these results shows that the main reasons for the Congress victory, despite poor vote share, were the division of the pro-Assamese nationalist votes between the AGP and NAGP and the unprecedented performance of the BJP. The Natun Asom Gana Parishad (NAGP), a breakaway faction of the AGP, won five seats with 5.5 percent votes. The CPI (M) won two and four seats went to CPI, in these elections. Among the parties representing ethnic minorities, the newly formed Autonomous State Demand Committee (ASDC) of Karbi Anglong district won four assembly seats with 1.6 percent votes. Other such parties drew a blank. The BJP, which was never a significant force before, won 10 seats and polled 6.4 percent votes. While the AGP and the NAGP together polled 23.6 percent. The BJP's 6.4 percent votes in 47 constituencies, spread all over the state, must have cut into the vote share of the non-Congress forces. **Therefore, the seats won by the Congress in 1991 need not necessarily mean an improvement in its support base. The decline that started in 1977 continued despite its being able to form a government in the state.**

Moreover, an analysis of the constituency-wise performance of the Congress Party shows that, in this election, Congress performance was much better in the areas dominated by the non-Assamese speaking population. Out of the 65 seats it won, at least 40 were constituencies where *'Ana-Asomiya'*, *'Na-Asomiya'*[5] or the tea garden labour population was electorally significant. At the parliamentary level, in 1985, the Congress won four seats out of a total of 14 with 23.5 percent votes and in 1991 it won eight seats with 28.5 percent votes. The AGP won a single seat with 17.6 votes. The NAGP could not win any seat but polled a significant 5.9 percent vote. Like its performance in the assembly elections, in the parliamentary elections too, the BJP won two seats with 9.6 percent votes. The scenario at the parliamentary level thus was not much different from that of the Assembly elections.

In the parliamentary elections of 1991, the Congress fared better in the areas dominated by tea garden labour and *Na-Asomiyas*. In the *Asomiya* areas it could win where it did, only because of a split in the *Asomiya* nationalist votes between the AGP and NAGP. In Dhubri, with a large immigrant population, the Congress polled 26.5 percent votes while the AGP and NAGP were nowhere near it, polling 7.4 percent and 2.4 percent respectively. The BJP, which was in the second position, polled a significant 19.6 percent. The Congress thus had a comfortable margin. In Jorhat, with a significant presence of tea garden labour, the Congress polled 44.9 percent while the AGP and NAGP polled 24.1 percent and 6.9 percent only, respectively. The Congress had a margin of almost 20 percent over the AGP and of almost 11 percent over AGP and NAGP put together. In another similar constituency Dibrugarh, the Congress polled 50.5 percent, AGP in the second place polled just 22 percent and NAGP came a poor third with 7.3 percent. The Congress again had a margin of over 30 percent. In Kaliabor, the Congress had a margin of about 10 percent over AGP and NAGP. It polled 45.6 percent, AGP 26.3 percent and NAGP 9.3 percent. In the Lakhimpur constituency, Congress got 31.4 percent, AGP could manage 21.1 percent and NAGP polled 1.9 percent thus giving Congress an edge of over 7 percent. In Tezpur, with a sizeable Nepali and tea labour population, the Congress polled 41.9 percent while the AGP polled 23.2 percent and the NAGP polled 10.9 percent. The Congress had about 7 percent advantage over the two regional parties. But in constituencies like Mangaldoi and Guwahati, where this non-Assamese factor was insignificant, it could not show similar strength. In Mangaldoi, it polled 24 percent, the AGP 21.4 percent and the NAGP 12.3 percent. The two regional parties together polled about 9 percent more than the Congress. In Guwahati, the Congress polled 23.8 percent, NAGP 17.5 percent and AGP polled 16.6 percent. The AGP and NAGP together polled 34.1 percent, 10.3 percent more than the Congress. Nowgong was the only constituency where this pattern did not emerge. Despite the presence of a sizeable immigrant population, the AGP won the seat with 24.4 percent vote. The NAGP polled 3 percent and the Congress polled just 22.3 percent. In this context it is important to keep in mind that Nowgong happens to be home district of one of the best known faces of the movement, Prafulla Kumar Mahanta, the then president of AASU. Therefore Nowgong was more of an exception. It is therefore clear that even at the parliamentary level election the Congress was experiencing an erosion of its support base and the regional forces were gaining ground over it. **Electoral politics of the state was thus becoming a sphere where *Asomiya* nationalist forces and the parties representing the interests of the smaller ethnic groups were beginning to challenge the Congress, the most dominant national party. An understanding of the Congress' decline is necessary for understanding the ascendance of regional and ethnic forces.**

The Shifting Support Base

It is well known that, in Assam during its period of inception, the Congress was thriving on the support of the *Asomiya* middle class and its predecessor, the newly emerging educated elite of the British days. In the pre-independence period, all its leaders were from the newly emerging western educated elite that took the shape of a middle class by the last decade of the 19th century.[6] H.K. Barpujari has pointed out that representatives from Assam had attended the early sessions of the Congress, including the first meeting that preceded its foundation. Barpujari also provides us with names of some of these representatives. Prominent among them were Debicharan Baruah, Gopinath Bordoloi, Kalikanta Barkakti, Satyanath Borah. All these gentlemen participated in the second session of the Congress. Radhanath Changkakoti and

Laksmikanta Barkakoti attended the third session.[7] A look at the names of the delegates from the Brahmaputra Valley to National Congress sessions from 1886 to 1921 shows that most of them belonged either to the middle class or its predecessor, the western educated elite[8]. In the *Asomiya* dominated areas of this valley, the Congress became its mouthpiece and generally articulated and tried to protect its interests by advocating the idea of an 'Assamese nationality'. This was reflected in the election promises of 1946 itself. A Congress election leaflet declared.

Unless the province of Assam be organised on the basis of the Assamese language and Assamese culture, the survival of the Assamese nationality and culture will become impossible. The inclusion of Bengali-speaking Sylhet and Cachar (plains portion) and the immigration and importation of lakhs of Bengali settlers on wastelands has been threatening to destroy the distinctness of Assam and has, in practice caused many disorders in its administration. For appropriate solution and redress of this big problem, the Congress Party should be installed as the majority party in the assembly.[9]

It is interesting to note that on the basis of such appeals, the Congress polled 48 percent votes in those elections. More importantly, it polled 78.3 percent in the general constituencies. The audience of this appeal obviously was the Assamese-speaking residents of the state who under the hegemony of the emerging educated middle class were growing in to a linguistic nationality, called the *Asomiya*.[10] The Congress could follow such a pro-Assamese nationalist policy in that period without much opposition primarily because the Surma valley was then not a part of Assam Congress. It was a part of the Bengal Congress. The immigrant population though substantial[11] was politically not well organised and the Assamese speaking population held sway over the politics of the state. The communities like the Bodos, Mishings and Karbis were yet to assert their identity. The Nagas had been demanding independence but the Khasi-Jaintias, Garos and Mizos were only beginning to understand parliamentary democracy. The Congress could therefore concentrate on winning the Assamese over to its side. The party could do that rather easily by raising the issue of national identity of the *Asomiya* because by that time the *Asomiya* middle class, for whom this issue was important, had ascended to hegemony.[12] The proof of the *Asomiya* middle classes' obsession with national identity is not difficult to find. Even in its nascent phase itself some leaders of this class had told the Congress that they would become ardent supporters of the Congress provided it took measures to protect the Assamese national identity.[13] It was therefore natural for the Congress to promise protection of this identity, defined in terms of Assamese language and culture, and thus to create a support base among the Asomiyas.

But after independence the support structure of the Congress Party in Assam underwent a change. Or rather it was forced to redefine its support base. A major Bengali-speaking area, namely Barak Valley, was now brought under the jurisdiction of the state of Assam and as a result Bengali population became electorally significant for Assam Congress. The *Asomiyas* and the Assamese Bengalis became the two most numerous linguistic groups of post-independence Assam. Right from the pre-British days, the elites of these two linguistic communities had been vying with each other for dominance over the land mass now known as Assam. As we have shown elsewhere, ever since mid nineteenth century, when Bengali was given the status of the language of court and schools, the *Asomiya* elite had become apprehensive of the intentions of the Bengali residents of Assam. The chauvinist section of the *Asomiya* middle class kept accusing all Bengali residents of Assam of expansionist designs and the chauvinist section of the Bengali residents of Assam and their patrons in Bengal openly expressed their desire to reduce the Asomiyas to a subjugated community in their own homeland.[14] During the early decades of the post-independence democratic politics we notice emergence of assertive educated elites in the smaller communities of the composite state of Assam and the *Asomiya* middle class hegemony coming under pressure from non-*Asomiya* forces. In such a situation, the Congress' earlier policy of standing for the protection of the *Asomiya* interest became politically inopportune. With the continuous influx of refugees from the erstwhile East Pakistan and with more and more tribal communities like the Khasis, Garos, Bodos trying to assert their own identities, the situation was becoming increasingly complicated. The *Asomiya* middle class, in the meantime, was becoming more aggressive. As was evident from the policies pursued by the Congress on issues like official language, medium of instruction and establishment of refineries, the Assam Pradesh Congress was trying to do some tight rope walking. But the central leadership of the party appeared to be insensitive to the problems of the state.

This insensitivity was becoming more and more pronounced. The Congress' attitudes towards the demands of the various groups like the hill tribes and the Bodos showed elements of uncertainty. For instance, when the Bodos demanded introduction of *Bodo* as the medium of instruction up to the secondary level, in the then Goalpara district in 1968, the then chief minister stated it to be contradictory to the government's educational policy.[15] The demand of a separate state made by the hill tribes like the Khasis, the Jaintias, and the Garos, which was articulated by the All Party Hill Leaders Conference (APHLC), too did not receive a sympathetic response in the beginning.[16] It is true that on the eve of elections the Congress always takes steps to gain popularity and tries to undo the damages caused by its policies. For instance, on the issues of the establishment of a second oil refinery in Assam and the demand of a separate hill state, the Assam Congress initially took courses of actions, which alienated large sections of the population who were supporting these demands. It tried to salvage the situation by announcing measures to placate these sections just before the elections.[17] Till the late sixties and early seventies the *Asomiya* middle class was still controlling the affairs of the state through the Congress Party and therefore such attitudes could be interpreted as the attitudes of the *Asomiya* middle class. Of course, there were tussles for leadership within the party leading to factional politics, which contributed to the erosion of its support structure. But these conflicts could not remain unaffected by the over all 'communal' rivalries.[18]

It is interesting to note that during the post-independence period when the Congress Party was losing its original support base for the reasons discussed above, some regional political groups and parties were emerging in Assam. Some of these, like the All Party Hill Leaders Conference (APHLC) with non-Assamese speaking ethnic support base, began to do fairly well. But the regional groups formed in the *Asomiya* areas like the Peoples Democratic Party and the *Ujani Assam Rajya Parishad* could not make any mark in the electoral politics of the state.[19] These election results were reflective of the *Asomiya* middle Class' hegemonic position in Assam politics. The regional forces in the *Asomiya* areas could become significant in the electoral arena only after the six-year long Assam agitation. It was under such circumstances that the compulsions of parliamentary politics seemed to have forced the Congress to concentrate on the most organised and insecure sections of the society in Assam — the tea garden labourers and the immigrant population. As K.M. Deka shows the rural Muslims and the tea-labour communities had a tendency of voting *en bloc* for the Congress. Assam has a large tea garden labour population and the only trade union organisation, which has been able to penetrate this section in Assam, till 1990s was the Indian National Trade Union Congress (INTUC). The Muslim immigrants have been insecure particularly in view of the aggressive posture of the *Asomiya* middle class. But because of their increasing number this community was becoming more and more relevant in electoral terms.[20] As we have shown above the election results of 1991 shows that the support base of the Congress has changed over the years and it has come to depend on the immigrants, tea garden labour and other *Ana-Asomiya* sections. Some deliberations in the Assam Pradesh Congress Committee show that the Congress has been concerned about its hold over these sections.[21]

Elections and Ethnic Politics

By 1996, the Assam Congress needed a new electoral strategy because on the one hand the unprecedented corruption and indiscriminate use of the repressive state machinery by the Hiteswar Saikia government alienated a large section of *Asomiyas* and on the other AGP and NAGP became united just before the elections to the Assembly and the Parliament. Moreover, other opposition parties including the left parties and even UMF — a party that had been claiming to represent the interests of the religious and linguistic minorities — joined hands with other regional forces. The situation was further complicated by the problem of extremist politics of organisations like the United Liberation Front of Asom (ULFA) and Bodo Security Force (BDSF). In early 1995, most observers would have agreed that the next elections would be fought on the issues of corruption and violation of democratic rights.[22] It was under such circumstances that the Congress tried to change the focus of politics to an issue, which could give it an advantage over others. In a clever move, Saikia sought to change the political discourse so that the issues of corruption and violation of democratic rights would recede to the background on the election eve. He tried to create conditions, which would ensure that the issue of ethnic identities in this multi-ethnic state gained vital importance in electoral politics. The articulate sections of the Bodos, the Karbis and the Mishings have been trying to mobilise 'their' people on ethnic lines. The Bodos and the Karbis had already been demanding political autonomy and their movements, like many such others, had acquired an anti-government character. Saikia was quick to realise that in a multi-ethnic state, if more tribal communities took to such movements, his party, with its high command generally viewing regional and ethnic aspiration as inimical to 'national integration', would become increasingly unpopular. The experiences of the Assam agitation in the late seventies were too recent to be forgotten. During the movement the Congress in Assamese speaking areas of the state got so isolated that "boycott Congress leaders" call given by the AASU made it impossible for party activists even to attend social functions like marriage and funerals. Saikia needed to fracture the electorate in Assam. He therefore, declared that his government would grant autonomy to all tribal communities. This move was directed at mobilising near total tribal support for his party. But two factors created serious problems for this strategy. One, the Congress' track record in keeping its word has been rather poor in Assam. The Assam Accord and the Bodo Accord remain only partly implemented. Tribal communities like the Lalungs, Rabhas, Mishings and the Bodos do not live in distinct areas where they are in a majority and therefore their autonomy would be without any defined territories. These factors made Saikia's promise appear empty. Some sections of these tribals, particularly some sections of their elites, realised this and the communities got divided. The anti-accord groups became so strong in communities like the Lalungs and the Mishings that in certain cases those leaders who supported the accords or signed such accords were not allowed to go back to their areas by their own communities. Another attempt at winning over some ethnic communities was the policy of granting scheduled tribe status to some of the communities who had been demanding such status. The Congress government's decision to grant ST status to the Koch Rajbangshis also ran into trouble because some ST communities were opposed to such a move. A Tribal Student Federation in fact filed a case in the Guwahati High Court against the decision to grant ST status to Koch Rajbangshis.[23] Congress could see that the *Asom Gana Parishad*, the main opposition party in Assam could remain a formidable force only if the *Asomiya* community could remain the single largest community in the Brahmaputra Valley. This was essentially a linguistic community that emerged during the six hundred years of *Ahom* rule from the early thirteenth to early nineteenth century. There was no doubt that the AGP, born out of the "Assam Movement" inspired by slogans like "*Jai Ai Asom*" derived its strength from the support of this linguistic community that embraced the smaller tribal communities of the Brahmaputra valley. But if the communities traditionally considered being parts of the *Asomiya* culture, like the Lalungs, Rabhas, Mishings, Koch Rajbangshis and even Ahoms, begin to distinguish themselves from the *Asomiya* identity then the AGP's support base would shrink. In such a situation it will have to be content with being a party of the small *Asomiya* community, comprising the caste Hindu Assamese speaking population, and may be a small section of the Assamese speaking Muslims of Upper Assam. Therefore Saikia plunged into a game of ethnic politics. But the Congress game plan failed primarily because of the lack of credibility of the party and its leadership and the united opposition's ability to keep the focus on corruption and violation of democratic rights. Organisations like the Committee for the Protection of Freedom of Expression (CPFE) and the Ganatantrik Adhikar Surakhya Samiti (GASS) formed by influential sections of the press, intellectuals and the non-Congress parties played an important role in maintaining that focus.

That state repression, corruption and ethnic identity remained crucial issues for the election became clear from the fact that almost all manifestos of the major non-Congress parties focussed on these issues. The AGP manifesto promised to bring an end to mal-administration and corruption. Autonomy and the problems of the tribal people of Assam are the other two issues, which it promised to solve if it came to power. The AGP manifesto also declared that the Constitution needed to be amended to grant autonomy to the states. It deplored the misuse of the army to repress ordinary people and promised a series of steps for the general development of the state.[24] The CPI (M) manifesto was more articulate in this context. In a section called 'The Situation in Assam', it accused the Congress government of letting lose a reign of terror in the name of controlling extremists. It also accused the Saikia government of sowing seeds of conflict among the Rabha, Tiwa and Mishing people in the name of granting autonomy. It identified the government as the instrument of massive corruption.[25] The CPI too identified corruption, repression and problems of nationalities as major issues.[26] The BJP included a section called 'Administration' in its manifesto, in which corruption and violation of democratic rights were highlighted. The problems of tribals and other backward sections also figured in the manifesto.[27] Even a small party, Peoples Democratic Front (PDF), representing Bodo ethnic identity, blamed the Saikia ministry of corruption, atrocities and of complicating ethnic problems.[28] It was interesting to note that except the BJP, none of the parties including the AGP really harped on the issue of the detection and deportation of 'foreigners' though most of them insisted that immigration from Bangladesh should be stopped. BJP was the only party, which advocated the pre-1985 AGP line. But this issue never really took off because its main vehicle, the AGP, decided to play it down, particularly because of the alliances it had to form to keep the non-Congress votes together. Saikia's attempt at diverting the attention of the electorate from these issues by playing ethnic politics,[29] in fact, boomeranged leading to divisions among communities like the Rabhas, Lalungs and Mishings and alienation of a large number of tribals from the Congress Party. Even BPP(P), its ally in the Bodo areas could not keep the focus on issues Saikia chose. The ethnic issue in fact remained live in the Bodo and Karbi areas but was monopolised by the anti-Congress UDF and ASDC.

Civil Society Intervention: Non-Congress Response to Ethnic Politics and Repression

While Saikia pursued politics of repression and ethnic division, the non-Congress opposition, at least the most influential sections of that began closing ranks and sought to intervene decisively in electoral politics. Newspaper reports, particularly in the regional press, beginning from 1994 showed that the non-Congress forces in Assam were getting together, initially on the issue of state repression. In mid-1994 itself Hiteswar Saikia's government was using the police and military forces to deal not only with the extremist elements but also more generally, with forces which were anti-government. The fourth estate came in for a real rough treatment. Journalists who reported the atrocities and those who began criticizing the corrupt practices of the government were becoming its targets. It was alleged that the police and the security forces were picking up even political leaders at the village, town and district levels, who were considered troublesome. The Terrorist and Disruptive Act (TADA) was being used almost indiscriminately to silence dissent. A section of journalists took the initiative and formed an organization called the Bak Swadhinata Surakhya Samiti or the Committee for the Protection of the Freedom of Expression (CPFE). A large number of leaders of non-Congress political parties participated in this mobilization. At the initiative of journalists and some leading intellectuals, a political platform called *Ganatantrik Adhikar Sangram Samiti* (GASS) was formed on September 6, 1994[30] at Guwahati. This organisation made its political position clear through a statement, issued in its first state convention, which highlighted the corrupt practices of the government, state repression, and also took clear positions on most of the live issues of politics in the state. It demanded protection of human rights, decentralization of political power, withdrawal of anti-people acts, implementation of the Assam accord and deportation of foreign immigrants with March 25, 1971 as the cut-off date, implementation of the Bodo accord and wanted steps for protection of the tribal people. It wanted the creation of an environment conducive to negotiations with the ULFA and the BDSF. It demanded release of all journalists detained under TADA. It further demanded that the natural resources of Assam be utilised in the interest of the residents of Assam. It opposed GATT and demanded measures to solve the economic problems of the people of the state. This platform received support from powerful student bodies like the All Assam Student Union (AASU) and the All Bodo Student Union (ABSU). The GASS ultimately took formal shape and contested municipal elections in Guwahati city. Though its electoral performance was poor, it made it possible for the non-Congress forces except BJP and small leftist parties like the SUCI and CPI (ML) to come together. The AGP and all major non-Congress political forces moved towards an understanding. This understanding culminated in an alliance of the five major parties — the AGP, the CPI, the CPI (M), the Autonomous State Demand Committee (ASDC) and the Bodo Peoples Party (Sangsuma) [BPP (S)]. There were efforts to bring the Janata Dal and the United

Minorities Front (UMF) also into the front. In the meantime the National Democratic Front (NDFB), a banned organization of Bodo militants, directed the Bodo political parties to unite so that the anti-Congress Bodo votes did not get divided. As a result, in the Bodo dominated areas, the BPP(S), the Plains Tribal Council of Assam (PTCA) and the United Democratic Front (UDF) decided to come together. The Bodo People's Party (Premsing) [BPP(P)] however, remained with the Congress. The United People's Party of Assam (UPPA), a party representing minority interests, too arrived at an understanding with the AGP. In the pre-election alliance formation of the non-Congress forces, the BJP was isolated. The Janata Dal kept a low profile. The Congress thus was without a major ally. It did forge an alliance of sorts with the BPP(P) in Bodo areas which could not actually improve its position. The major sections of the left, the regional forces and the ethnic and religious minorities stood solidly behind the AGP-led alliance. It became clear that the politics of divisiveness, corruption and repression followed by Congress under Hiteswar Saikia's leadership became the most difficult electoral disadvantage.

The Boomerang

The boomerang effect of Saikia's repressive and divisive politics became clear because the most significant political outcome of this was the coming together of the AGP, CPI and CPI(M). From the beginning of the Assam agitation of the late seventies, the left parties and the forces behind AGP had been at loggerheads. The agitation, because of its focus on Bengali immigrants from Bangladesh, came to be viewed as anti-Bengali and that forced the left with its strong Bengali connections to fight the agitators. The left parties also opposed the agitation on ideological grounds. Commenting on the character of the movement, Assam's most well known leftist intellectual Hiren Gohain (1980) wrote, "Several leaders of the AASU and the Assam Jatiyatabadi Dal (sic) have made incendiary speeches inciting violence against leftists and 'traitors'.... A particularly revealing side-light has been the decisive anti-left orientation of the movement."[31] But the experience of five years in power and five years in opposition seemed to have helped AGP to learn some lessons. It realised that it could not rule Assam without securing the support of the *Ana-Asomiya* population. Its silence, on the issue of detection and deportation of immigrants, during the campaign period as reflected in its manifesto indicated this realization. The alliance with the major left parties was therefore not a surprise. Saikia government's corrupt image and the repressive tactics became catalysts to this development.

The alliance, as we shall see in another section dealing with poll analysis, benefited the AGP most. In the Barak Valley, where in 1985 it could not win a single seat in the assembly elections it won two seats with big margins. The AGP supported UPPA won another seat in the same area. By preventing the splitting of anti-Congress votes, the alliance proved to be most advantageous to the main non-Congress Party and the main opposition in the previous assembly, namely the AGP, and not only in the assembly elections but also in parliamentary elections.

The isolation of the Congress and its inability to keep the focus on the issues on hand seriously affected its prospects. As shown in Table 3, in the Lok Sabha elections the Congress and the AGP won five seats each. One seat went to an independent candidate. Compared to 1991 (Table 3) the Congress lost three seats, and the

Table 3: Assam Election Results (1989–98)

		Lok Sabha Elections				Vidhan Sabha Elections	
Year		1989*	1991	1996	1998	1991	1996**
Total Seats		–	14	14	14	126	126
Turn Out %		–	75.3	78.5	61.1	75.7	78.9
INC	Seats	–	8	5	10	66	34
	Vote	–	28.5	31.6	38.97	29.2	30.6
AGP	Seats	–	1	5	–	19	59
	Vote	–	17.6	27.2	12.72	17.9	29.7
BJP	Seats	–	2	1	1	10	4
	Vote	–	9.6	15.9	24.47	6.7	10.4
CPI	Seats	–	–	–	–	4	3
	Vote	–	2.1	–	0.95	2.5	2.0
CPI (M)	Seats	–	1	1	–	2	2
	Vote	–	4.7	3.9	3.27	3.9	1.9
JD	Seats	–	–	–	–	1	–
	Vote	–	5.2	0.7	0.12	4.8	0.6
Others	Seats	–	1	1	2	9	9
	Vote	–	18.0	9.0	10.18	10.6	7.4
Ind	Seats	–	1	1	1	15	11
	Vote	–	14.3	11.7	9.51	24.4	17.4

Source: Election Department, Government of Assam.

* Elections were not held.

** Elections countermanded for four seats.

BJP lost one. The AGP gained four seats. The CPI (M), ASDC and independents retained their one seat each. Compared to the 1991 elections, the Congress lost four seats to the AGP but it won one seat from the BJP. Thus the Congress' loss was AGP's gain. Two of these seats, Guwahati and Mangaldoi were constituencies where the *Asomiya* regional sentiments were predominant and where traditional Congress supporters like the immigrants and the tea-garden labour were absent. Two other constituencies, Kaliabor and Lakhimpur, had significant tea-labour population. AGP's victory in these two constituencies showed a decline of Congress influence among the tea-labour. But the AGP candidates won these seats with narrow margins. In Kaliabor, the Congress got 37.7 percent votes while the AGP polled 37.9 percent. In Lakhimpur, the Congress polled 32.5 percent and the AGP polled 33.5 percent. The Congress with significant margins retained two other tea-labour dominated constituencies, Dibrugarh and Jorhat. It polled 50.6 percent in Dibrugarh while the AGP polled only 31.3 percent. In Jorhat, it polled 48 percent while the AGP polled 40.7 percent.

The isolation however did not seem to affect Congress' hold in one community in a traditional a support base. It seemed to retain its influence among the immigrants. It retained Dhubri seat with 40.1 percent while the AGP polled 23.2 percent in the constituency. The BJP's influence in the Barak Valley, dominated by the non-Assamese population, was on the decline but it was not out. The Congress won the Silchar seat from the BJP with 42.7 percent, but the latter did poll a significant 30.5 percent votes. In the Autonomous (ST) seat in Karbi Anglong, ASDC polled 52.7 percent while the Congress polled only 22.5 percent. The CPI (M) retained the Barpeta seat with 36.8 percent. The Congress polled only 15 percent and BJP polled another 14.9 percent.

The unity of the major non-Congress parties of regional, leftist and ethnic orientations played a decisive role, particularly in the tribal-dominated areas of the state (Table 5). These areas had been traditional Congress bastions in which the party could dominate till 1985. But in this election the non-Congress alliance could defeat the party in constituencies like Baithalangsu, Halflong, Diphu, Gossaigaon, Sidli and Udalguri.[32] In this area, comprising 14 assembly constituencies, 11 seats went to parties representing respective tribal communities. Two seats went to the AGP. The

Table 4: Percentage of Votes Polled by Parties in Lok Sabha Elections (1996)

Constituency	INC	BJP	AGP	CPI (M)	ASDC	JD	INC (T)	CPI (ML)	IND
Karimganj (SC)	28.2	33.1	27.1	–	–	2.1	0.6	–	–
Silchar	42.7	30.5	–	21.7	52.7	–	0.6	–	–
Autonomous (ST)	22.5	3.0	–	–	–	–	–	–	–
Dhubri	40.1	21.8	23.2	–	–	–	5.5	–	–
Kokrajhar (ST)	16.9	16.1	20.1	–	–	–	–	–	24.4
Barpeta	15.0	14.9	–	36.8	–	–	2.7	–	–
Gauhati	30.7	19.4	44.3	–	–	–	0.5	–	–
Mangaldoi	20.7	15.6	33.2	–	–	1.1	1.3	–	–
Tezpur	32.5	13.0	31.4	–	–	2.3	6.2	–	–
Nowgong	28.7	20.1	36.1	–	–	–	1.4	–	–
Kaliabor	37.7	5.5	37.9	–	–	1.4	15.7	–	–
Jorhat	48.0	5.6	40.7	–	–	–	4.3	–	–
Dibrugarh	50.6	8.5	31.3	–	–	–	3.3	2.0	–
Lakhimpur	32.5	8.5	33.1	–	–	1.9	3.8	–	–

Source: Calculated from Election Commission of India.

Table 5: Voting Pattern in Tribal Dominated Areas in Vidhan Sabha Elections, 1996

Constituency	Votes Polled By Parties (Percent)								
	Turn out	INC	AGP	BJP	INC (T)	ASDC	PDF	BSMC	Ind
Halflong (ST)	78.6	33.3	–	–	6.3	54.6	–	–	5.8
Bokajan (ST)	82.6	15.9	–	–	–	57.9	–	–	23.1
Howraghat (ST)	86.4	18.7	–	1.1	–	54.2	–	–	261.0
Diphu (ST)	80.1	24.6	–	4.3	–	41.8	–	–	29.1
Baithalangso (ST)	75.0	40.1		4.4		55.6	–	–	–
Gossaingaon	87.2	27.0	36.9	9.5	–	–	–	–	11.5
Kokrajhar West (ST)	87.2	11.2	9.0	9.8		–	13.2	27.6	2.6
Kokrajhar East (ST)	83.1	12.4	10.7	7.8		–	21.4	45.1	7.7
Sidli (ST)	79.8	14.0	–	9.6	–	–	32.6	28.7	26.2
Kalaigaon	80.9	21.2	29.2	8.9	4.1	–	–	–	–
Udalguri	77.9	47.6	–	–	–	–	52.4	–	
Bijni	84.4	15.8	26.0	9.5	0.5	–	40.6	–	2.5
Panery	80.2	28.4	25.2	2.9	0.7	–	42.0	–	0.8
Tamulpur	80.0	16.9	24.0	4.6	9.9	–	33.1	–	7.3

Source: Calculated from Election Commission of India.

Congress drew a blank. In the Karbi areas, ASDC won all the five seats. In the Bodo areas, independents owing allegiance to the various Bodo factions, who were part of the non-Congress opposition, won seven seats and AGP won the other two seats. In the Karbi areas ASDC's margin over the Congress was so high that the latter appeared to be losing its electoral significance. In Halflong, the margin was 13,671, in Bokajan it was 26,843. In Howraghat, the Congress did not have a candidate of its own but the independent candidate lost to ASDC by 8,495 votes. In Baithalangsu, the Congress lost by a margin of 13,325 votes. In the Bodo areas the winning margins were not very high because of the fact that in those areas no dominant tribal party emerged and the tribal votes thus were divided. But the mood was anti-Congress. **The results of this election exposed the myth that in Assam, the Congress influence over tribals was significant.**

In the immigrant areas[33] also the alliance proved to be effective. As Table 6 shows in these areas, out of a total of 15 seats, the Congress won four, AGP four, CPI (M) two, UMF two CPI one, Congress (T) one and PDF won one seat. Thus the AGP and the Congress did equally well. Even their vote share remained more or less equal. It is interesting to note that the UMF claiming to represent minority interests and particularly immigrant minority interests could win only two seats in this region.

Newspaper reports during the run up to the elections show that the Congress was trying to mobilise religious minorities, a

Table 6: Voting Pattern in Immigrant Areas in the Vidhan Sabha Elections, 1996

Constituency	Turnout	INC	AGP	BJP	UMF	CPI (M)	CPI	INC (T)	IND
Barpeta	80.9	4.1	29.5	7.0	–	–	–	32.5	16.5
Sarbhog	85.1	16.5	–	10.4	–	43.7	–	6.3	12.9
Jania	88.1	7.0	–	1.1	21.3	13.6	–	2.9	20.1
Bagber	89.3	26.7	25.3	–	39.7	–	–	2.5	1.2
Sarukhetri	81.3	11.9	–	4.4	11.9	28.5	–	16.1	10.9
Chenga	85.4	32.3	25.8	5.3	–	–	–	10.2	20.7
Mangaidoi (SC)	80.6	34.0	42.1	9.8	6.5	–	–	1.0	4.9
Hojai	79.7	40.3	34.9	22.5	–	–	–	0.3	15.9
Jamunamukh	80.1	26.3	38.7	7.4	–	–	2.8	0.3	15.9
Man Kachar	89.5	46.5	48.8	0.8	–	–	–	0.2	3.4
South Salmara	89.9	59.7	4.5	–	–	–	–	3.7	23.2
Bilasipara east	85.4	38.0	42.3	11.1	–	–	–	0.4	2.2
Bilasipara west	88.3	21.7	–	21.0	–	–	22.4	26.0	2.2
Dhubri	85.2	39.1	–	30.4	–	22.6	–	3.3	3.0
Gauripur	88.1	28.6	14.9	16.9	–	–	–	1.6	32.1

Source: Calculated from Election Commission of India.

large majority of whom were immigrants, by activating its minority cell. It also tried to keep the UMF leaders with it. But the riots that took place in many religious minorities inhabited areas and the general aversion to communal violence seemed to have created a serious situation. The Jamate-Islami's All India President Arsad Madani had to send his brother to campaign for AGP.[34] The experience of the five years of AGP rule, when there were no riots and when no real attempts were made to deport the immigrant settlers of the 'chars' must have motivated the immigrant population to try its luck with the front. The UMF's failure to make an impact could be understood in terms of the general feeling among Assam voters that political parties do not care specially for particular communities. During the post-poll survey for 1996 elections, conducted by the CSDS, when respondents were asked whether they had a particular party, which specially cared for them, 85.9 percent said they did not have such a party while only 5.7 percent thought that there was such a party.

The tea-belt[35] has often been held as a preserve of the Congress[36] and during the preceding decade, the Congress Party had been able to retain its hold over the voters of this region, i.e. the constituencies dominated by the tea-labour community. Even during the AGP's wave in 1985 these voters helped the Congress to win the Dibrugarh parliamentary seat comfortably. In the 1996 assembly elections of the total of 30 such tea-labour dominated constituencies the Congress won 16, AGP won 13 and CPI won one seat. The AGP seems to have thus made inroads into the Congress bastion in the tea labour dominated constituencies (Table 7).

Assam *Chah Mazdoor Sangha*, an affiliate of INTUC has been organizing the tea-labour of Assam since 1947. The organizational strength of INTUC in the tea belt of the Brahmaputra Valley had been one of the reasons for Congress dominance in this region.[37] The situation seems to have changed radically by 1990s. The BJP, CPI and the AGP have been trying to find a foothold in this region. The AGP in fact, had started the Assam Chah Shramik Parishad to counter the INTUC. In Chabua area 15,000 tea workers were reported to have left the INTUC controlled Assam Chah Mazdoor Sangha to join Assam Chah Shramik Parishad.[38] The AASU too has been trying to influence the Tea Tribal Student Organisation for quite some time now. In a community where the large majority

Table 7: Voting Pattern in Tea Growing Areas in Vidhan Sabha Elections, 1996

Name of Constituency	Turn-out	Percentage of Votes Polled by						
		INC	AGP	BJP	CPI(M)	CPI	INC(T)	IND
Dhekiajuli	80.4	33.7	46.4	10.7	–	–	1.1	7.9
Berchallar	81.3	33.0	39.3	6.5	–	–	1.0	5.7
Tezpur	75.8	42.0	44.7	10.9	–	–	2.0	0.3
Rangapara	80.2	47.7	–	8.4	27.0	–	5.3	7.8
Sootea	81.1	13.0	40.9	1.9	–	–	10.0	23.3
Biswanath	81.6	31.8	42.7	15.7	–	–	9.0	0.4
Behali	79.8	33.4	18.9	8.9	–	–	9.1	4.3
Gohpur	77.0	33.9	36.8	4.2	–	–	11.7	5.0
Lakhimpur	77.3	23.9	44.7	6.1	–	–	2.1	11.1
Koliabor	79.4	36.2	47.2	8.0	–	–	4.5	4.1
Golaghat	77.1	34.8	48.7	1.6	–	–	6.9	–
Khumtai	76.0	26.2	26.9	1.5	–	–	4.0	36.8
Dibrugarh	66.2	40.7	29.9	18.3	–	–	7.0	1.4
Lahowal	71.3	50.4	39.9	1.8	–	25.7	5.0	1.4
Duliajan	67.3	47.8	–	12.3	–	–	8.4	2.2
Tingkhong	74.9	44.9	41.8	1.4	–	–	1.1	4.3
Naharkatia	71.7	44.1	–	8.5	35.3	–	1.4	4.8
Chabua	73.4	38.1	39.4	2.9	–	–	15.6	1.3
Tinsukia	69.9	55.2	21.8	14.0	–	–	3.0	2.0
Doomdooma	68.9	67.2	17.5	6.5	–	–	5.6	1.0
Margherita	–	–	–	–	–	–	–	–
Sadia	73.5	32.9	40.0	–	–	–	10.5	3.2
Digboi	70.0	62.0	–	11.3	–	13.2	2.0	–
Moran	72.3	45.4	45.0	2.4	–	–	3.1	–
Mariani	71.0	46.2	36.8	9.4	–	–	3.6	1.2
Sonari	78.6	61.8	24.5	7.3	–	–	1.8	–
Thowra	75.9	29.4	10.8	1.8	–	11.5	11.4	21.5
Sibsagar	70.1	44.1	–	3.1	–	47.9	0.7	3.2
Bokaghat	74.1	36.8	34.5	2.7	–	–	2.5	17.8

Source: Calculated from Election Commission of India.

of people are poor and illiterate, students can play a decisive role. This factor has influenced the results of this election. In the assembly elections, the AGP won the Chabua seat though with a small margin. The myth of the Congress invincibility in the tea-belt stood exploded.

Persistent Issues

The newly emerging issues in electoral politics and their effect should not be viewed as temporary aberrations. The issues continued but the party in the receiving end changed. In 1998 the AGP's support base proved to be fragile. A complete reversal of the electoral reality unfolded and like Congress in the last election it was AGP that now faced the music. But the reasons were obvious! People expected, AGP to oppose state terrorism because of its own experiences during the Assam agitation. But despite the commitments made in the election manifesto, the AGP government imposed repressive measures, similar in form and content to those followed by Congress ministry establishing a virtual Army rule in Assam. This led to the alienation of the Assamese middle class from AGP. The performance of the government was so poor that even a normal obligation like payment of salaries to employees, including school teachers, release of funds for institutions of higher learning like universities could not be fulfilled. A bitter confrontation of the government with the major teahouses like the Tatas over the issue of harbouring extremists took place. The Government found evidence of Tata Tea's harbouring extremists but its handling of the situation reflected political immaturity. The attempts of the tea groups to placate the ultras were understandable, particularly in view of the growing power of the extremist groups in the state during the preceding few years. But the government's failure to provide security to the industry that was so vital to its economy definitely eroded its credibility. This confrontation with tea lobby had drained a lot of energy and time, when pressing problems like extremist violence, ethnic conflicts and infiltration plagued the state.[39] Corruption once again became a major issue. The Letter of Credit (LoC) scandal involving more than hundred of crores of rupees in which several ministers of earlier government as well as the incumbent ministry including its chief minister together with a host of government officials were implicated rocked the state. This provided the opposition a powerful plank in the election campaign against AGP. The call of some extremist groups to the people to keep away from electoral process had further added to the uncertainty and confusion prevailing in the state.[40] To make the matter worse, the killing of a close aide of AGP president, in Nowgong by ULFA, instilled fear among the workers of political parties. The ULFA's call to the people to boycott the polls this time came as a surprise as the extremist outfit in the earlier elections did not issue such a dictat. In fact, the 1991 and 1996 polls had passed off without interference with the fundamental rights of the people.[41] The situation was further complicated for the AGP by the fact that unlike, in 1996, smaller ethnic and religious parties like the ASDC, the PDF and United Minority Front did not join hands with AGP in this election. The coming together of the tribal groups like the Autonomous State Demand Committee, Mishing Mimang Kebang Autonomous Demand Struggling Front and the Karbi Anglong unit of the CPI (ML) under the banner of Assam People's Front was significant for electoral politics in Assam. The AGP stood alienated from the tribal electorate. Another problem the party faced was factional politics, leading to the exit of Bhrigu Kumar Phukan, the former AASU general secretary and the most important leader of the Assam movement and the formation of *Asom Jatiya Parishad*.

The problems of insurgency, corruption, ethnic identity, repeal of IMDT Act and stability constituted the main plank for election propaganda in 1998 Lok Sabha elections. Most of the manifestos had focused on these issues. But the parties did not have answers to the problems related to the issues they raised. The BJP manifesto came out with a statement on how the party proposed to tackle the two crying problems of the state: illegal infiltration from Bangladesh and the problem of insurgency. In a section called 'North-East' in its manifesto, the BJP blamed the Congress government for its failure to check the illegal migrants. It attributed this failure to Congress' lack of political will caused by its narrow and selfish interest. Further, it promised to repeal the Illegal Migrants Determination by Tribunal Act (IMDTA) and strengthen existing immigration laws and rules and enact new ones to make illegal infiltration difficult. It promised to deny the extension of benefits of citizenship to illegal immigrants.[42] The manifesto, however, did not seem to reflect a realisation that creating more laws, even strong ones, might not help stop illegal immigration because illegal acts are committed not because of absence of laws but because of non-implementation of laws. The party appeared to have promised to deal with the problem of unabated infiltration from across the border, apparently with an eye on the electorate in Assam. To be in tune with the aspirations generated by the 'Assam Agitation' over the Foreigner's issue it promised to maintain a National Register of Citizens.

The Congress (I) campaign concentrated on the stability plank.[43] In a separate manifesto on Assam, it promised to undertake or execute certain schemes like preparing a master plan for flood control in the Brahmaputra and Barak Valley. In the second part, the manifesto listed a number of schemes for implementation. The manifesto favoured a peaceful solution to the burning insurgency problem in the state. It also demanded the shifting of the Oil India and Tea Garden Headquarters to the state. This issue had been raised repeatedly by opinion builders of all hues in Assam because the state seemed to have lost considerable revenue because many companies operating in Assam had head offices out side the state. In the economic front the manifesto called for a separate economic policy for the North-Eastern region in order to create avenues of employment for the unemployed youth. Further, it emphasised the preparation of a correct voters' list.

The main plank of the United Front campaign was the development of Assam. United Front leaders reminded the people that Assam had received a raw deal from the centre when the Congress was in power for more than four and half decades of independence. It claimed that it was the UF government that gave top priority to the development of Assam and rest of the north-eastern region. The Assam People's Front (APF), a combine of ASDC, ADSF and CPI (ML) promised to continue with its relentless efforts to form a strong regional force to fight corrupt AGP, Congress (I) and fascist BJP in the state. APF leader Haliram Terang maintained that all these anti-people forces could be resisted only through United People's movement.[44] The party had fielded candidates in five Lok Sabha constituencies.

Assam Jatio Sanmilon in its manifesto focused on the issues of correct voters list up to 2000, Repeal of IMDT Act, solution of the unemployment problem, flood control and a corruption free state. The Autonomous State Demand Committee (ASDC), on the other hand revived its demand for an autonomous state. Further, ASDC and PDF have jointly called upon the people of the state to side with the forces opposed to Congress, BJP and AGP. The ethnic issue in fact remained the focal point of ASDC manifesto. Thus corruption, political autonomy and cultural identity of smaller communities, State repression, immigration and development remained major issues in the campaign. But corruption and ethnic identity seemed to over shadow all other issues.

The Lok Sabha election 1998 was held in the midst of calls by militant organizations, namely the ULFA and Bodo extremists, for boycott of the elections. In view of their influence among the rural masses it was no surprising that the voters turn out was low in the *Asomiya* dominated areas[45] of the state. The ULFA's poll boycott call greatly demoralized the *Asomiya* voters, and as a result the AGP suffered because, as a party emerging out of the Assam Agitation, that section of the voters was its main support base. A Post Poll Survey conducted by CSDS[46] found that the electioneering was on a very low key. The survey indicated low intensity of canvassing and voters' participation in the poll campaign [Table 8 (a) and 8 (b)]. The boycott call appeared to be instrumental in tilting the balance in favour of Congress which capitalised in its known strength of mobilizing voters in minority pockets and areas dominated by tea workers.[47] While during this period the electoral base of the Congress was shrinking in many states in India, it appeared to have been able to maintain part of its electoral base in Assam. The party polled 38.9 percent of votes and gained ten seats and its ally, the United Minority Front won one seat. The AGP and its allies, CPI (M) and CPI contested 12 seats but failed to retain even one of the five seats it held in the last election. The BJP emerged as an important electoral force and increased its vote share. Smaller parties reflecting the ethnic and religious identities namely ASDC, UMF supported by Congress and an independent candidate supported by ABSU could retain one seat each (Table 3). On the whole the mandate was against AGP led alliance and also indicative of decline of AGP's support

Table 8(a): Intensity of Canvassing

	No	Yes	DK
Up to 25 years	86.7	11.1	2.2
26–35 years	90.5	9.5	–
36–45 years	96.4	3.6	–
46–55 years	97.3	–	2.7
Above 56 years	93.9	6.1	–

Source: Post Poll Election Survey 1996 Conducted by CSDS.

Table 8(b): Campaign Participation

	No	Yes
Up to 25 years	97.8	1
26–35 years	96.8	3.2
36–45 years	100.0	–
46–55 years	100.0	–

Source: Post Poll Election Survey 1996 Conducted by CSDS.

among scheduled castes and scheduled tribes. A comparative analysis of surveys of 1996 and 1998 Lok Sabha elections (Tables 9 and 10) by CSDS indicated the changing pattern of support base of different parties. It appeared from the surveys that the support of AGP and allies among the Muslims went down to 13.4 percent in this election from 47.3 percent in 1996. On the other hand the support for the Congress among the Muslim went up to 75.6 percent as against 50 percent in 1996. While support for the BJP among Muslims remained unchanged. The acceptance of BJP is shown by substantial gains in support from groups that had previously shunned it, e.g., the scheduled castes. The BJP has also increased its base among scheduled tribes and OBCs. The increase in its base among SCs and STs came at the cost of AGP. Probably an explanation of this phenomenon could be found in AGP's general failure to retain its bases because of its inept handling of political matters and also in the lack of commitment of its leadership to its declared policies.

Table 9: Lok Sabha Elections, Assam 1996: Who Voted for Whom

	INC	BJP	AGP and Allies	Others
Age				
25 years and below	26.2	19.0	54.8	0.0
26–35 years	25.8	25.8	47.0	1.5
36–45 years	46.9	10.2	38.8	4.1
46–55 years	36.0	16.0	48.0	0.0
56 years and above	38.5	19.2	42.3	0.0
Gender				
Male	36.1	17.2	44.3	2.5
Female	29.9	21.8	48.3	0.0
Education				
Illiterate	41.6	20.2	36.0	2.2
Primary and Middle	33.3	13.7	51.0	2.0
Intermediate	24.1	16.7	59.3	0.0
Graduate and above	20.0	40.0	40.0	0.0
Caste				
Scheduled caste	22.1	11.1	66.7	0.0
Scheduled tribe	38.1	19.0	33.3	9.5
OBC	27.1	27.1	44.7	1.2
Others	39.4	12.8	47.9	0.0
Religion				
Hindu	23.4	28.9	46.1	1.6
Muslim	50.0	2.7	47.3	0.0

Source: Post Poll Election Survey 1996 Conducted by CSDS.

Table 10: Lok Sabha Elections, Assam 1998: Who Voted for Whom

	INC	BJP	AGP and Allies	Others
Age				
25 years and below	41.2	35.3	20.6	2.9
26–35 years	49.3	29.6	12.7	8.5
36–45 years	64.4	26.7	4.4	4.4
46–55 years	66.7	19.0	14.3	–
56 years and above	63.0	14.8	7.4	14.8
Gender				
Male	57.4	24.3	12.2	6.1
Female	51.4	30.1	10.8	7.2
Education				
Illiterate	62.5	26.1	4.5	6.8
Primary School	59.0	25.6	10.3	5.1
Middle School	45.5	27.3	18.2	9.1
High School	46.7	20.0	20.0	13.3
College no Degree	39.1	26.1	30.4	4.3
Graduate and above	25.0	50.0	25.0	–
Caste				
Scheduled caste	50.0	50.0	0.0	0.0
Scheduled tribe	25.0	37.5	25.0	12.5
OBC	45.2	38.7	14.0	2.2
Others	68.1	12.1	8.8	11.0
Religion				
Hindu	41.2	42.9	13.4	2.5
Muslim	75.6	2.6	9.0	12.8

Source: Post Poll Election Survey 1998 Conducted by CSDS.

Shifting Loyalties and Regaining Support

Loyalties seem to be shifting in Assam politics or rather vote banks of parties seem to be dissolving. The traditional strong holds seem to be disappearing with voters exercising options more judiciously. In late 1990s a churning seems to have taken place. By 1998 AGP's dent in the Congress strongholds appeared to be temporary. A significant shift of tea garden labour and immigrant Muslim votes back to the Congress and caste Hindu votes to BJP led to AGP's debacle in the Lok Sabha election. The Congress could retain Dibrugarh and Jorhat tea garden labour dominated Lok Sabha seats by polling as high as 64 to 65 percent of votes. The BJP was also successful to a great extent to find a foot hold in this region. It increased its base among tea community at the cost of AGP. The confrontation and bitterness that developed between AGP and the major tea houses might have facilitated entry of BJP among the tea community. But the fact remains that events preceding the elections deflected their electoral preference away from AGP and closer to the Congress.[48] Moreover, during the preceding decades a few new political leaders emerged among the tea communities, several of whom occupied very responsible positions in the Congress ministry and enjoyed considerable political clout. No such leaders in this community had emerged among the supporters of other political parties including AGP. Even the student leaders of the tea community who were parts of the Assam movement shifted ground. INTUC, the oldest labour organisation having allegiance to Congress contributed significantly in affecting the swing towards the Congress.

Election results of the immigrant-dominated constituencies also went in favour of Congress. Interestingly, a sizeable portion of minority Muslims who sided with AGP and allies in the last election shifted to Congress this time. The Congress retained all the seats in these areas by polling high percentages of votes. The major reason for this change might have been the apprehensions in the minds of minority community that in the event of BJP forming the government at the centre it would certainly repeal the IMDT Act, which in turn might adversely affect the interest of immigrant religious minority.[49] Further, the minorities seemed to have lost their trust on AGP for its mysterious silence over the issue, particularly when, AASU urged the centre and the state government to delete the names of those voters marked as 'doubtful' in the electoral roll published in 1997 and to repeal the IMDT Act.[50] Having experienced the clout of this student organization during the period of the "Assam Movement" immigrant Muslim population of Assam must have been thought it prudent to support Congress. It was apparent from the election results that the religious minorities rallied on the side of the Congress and the immigrant linguistic Hindu minority as well as a small portion of indigenous people supported BJP. But the shift of the minority support was to be seen in the context of the position of the UMF. The UMF, which could poll only 26.7 percent of votes in the constituencies it contested in the elections of 1996, was now catapulted to a position where it could muster the support of 58.64 percent of the voters in the relevant constituencies. Commentators pointed out that Hindu polarization in Assam invariably consolidated the Muslim voters in a more organized way.[51] The rise of BJP in religious minority dominant constituencies namely Dhubri, Nagaon and Barpeta only helped parties like Congress and UMF (Table 11) because it cut into AGP votes.

Table 11: Lok Sabha Elections 1998: Regionwise Performance

Constituency	Parties								
	INC	BJP	AGP	CPI(M)	CPI	ASDC	UMF	JD	IND
Karimganj	39.70	38.20	19.70	–	–	–	–	–	–
Silchar	33.80	37.05	–	27.70	–	–	–	–	–
Autonomous (ST)	20.20	12.00	–	–	–	47.08	–	–	–
Dhubri	50.04	24.10	–	–	10.50	–	–	–	–
Kokrajhar (ST)	11.80	15.30	6.30	–	–	–	–	–	25.55
Barpeta	–	21.80	–	16.50	–	–	58.64	–	–
Guwahati	49.57	27.30	21.40	–	–	–	–	–	–
Mangaldoi	41.78	22.19	18.30	–	–	–	–	–	–
Tezpur	45.15	24.60	21.60	–	–	–	–	–	–
Nowgong	42.10	36.10	16.80	–	–	–	–	–	–
Kaliabor	59.87	15.80	23.60	–	–	–	–	–	–
Jorhat	65.13	14.30	16.37	–	–	–	–	2.94	–
Dibrugarh	64.40	25.50	8.20	–	–	–	–	–	–
Lakhimpur	40.05	19.40	22.05	–	–	–	–	–	–

Source: Election Department, Government of Assam.

Congress' weakness in tribal dominated constituencies continued even in the 1998 Lok Sabha elections. The massive turn out of voters in these constituencies in spite of a poll boycott call given by extremist out-fits indicated the prevailing assertive behaviour of the tribal electorate and the strength of mobilization on ethnic line. It also indicates that in the number game of parliamentary politics smaller communities find it opportune to mobilize their people on ethnic lines. In the post independence period, the state of India has been offering protection to the tribal communities under the policy of protective discrimination. Despite such policies the tribals have perpetually experienced the problem of land alienation, poverty, indebtedness, severe unemployment, economic exploitation and cultural exploitation. The policy of protective discrimination has been able to create conditions only for the emergence of highly educated tribal elites in various tribal communities. These elites have learnt to play the game of numbers in electoral politics to pursue their interest but like most other educated elites in backward areas they paid scant regard to the interests of the masses of their respective communities. In northeast

India these elite have been at the fore front of the autonomy movements of the tribal communities. The tribal movements demanding creation of Udayachal, Bodoland and an autonomous tribal state in the hills continued to gain ground. The tribal parties espousing such causes remained popular in many tribal areas because these elites continued to be hegemonic forces in their respective communities, particularly in the absence of other important social forces. In the Karbi dominated autonomous parliamentary constituency the ASDC candidate Jayanta Rongpi was elected to the parliament for the fourth consecutive term and its margin over Congress was quite high. The BJP increased its vote share on these areas from 3.06 to 12.00 in 1998. In the Bodo areas, however, the winning margins were not high as no dominant Bodo leader emerged. Sansuma Khungur Bwismuthiary backed by ABSU won the election by polling 25.5 percent of votes while Congress candidate Premsingh Brahma, former militant Bodo leader, could poll only 11.8 percent of votes. Vote share of AGP candidate went down significantly as it could poll only 6.3 percent of votes. BJP's vote share remained at 15.3 percent. The election results in these areas clearly reflected the ethnic polarisation as well as ethnic accommodation.

Ducking the Issues

Corruption and repression remained the essential tools of governance even during this period. And in the run up to the elections the burden of incumbency began to prove too heavy for the ruling party. It therefore tried to duck the issues and deflect criticism by invoking a hackneyed conspiracy theory. The 1999 elections were preceded by some disquieting developments. There was a spate of news about Pakistani Inter Services Intelligence (ISI) conspiracies and intrigues in Assam in the local newspapers. Certain news about the possible links between the ISI and Muslim fundamentalist forces and ISI's plan to destabilize the State that appeared in the media just before election caused widespread unease and fear among the people in the State.[52] The state machinery appeared to be responsible for spreading such rumours. Even the Chief Minister himself made such a statement claiming that the *Madrasas* were the hotbeds of ISI intrigues in Assam. The decision of *Assam Jatiyatabadi Yuba Parishad*, an influential youth organization, perceived by some scholars as being close to ULFA, to form a new regional party called *Assam Gana Sangram Parishad* added a new dimension to the regional political scenario of Assam. The aim of the proposed party to stand as a political alternative to uphold and rejuvenate regionalism in the state was a direct challenge to the ruling *Asom Gana Parishad*. The formation of an alternative regional party was crucial in deciding the fortunes of regional forces, particularly, in view of the highly polarised demographic pattern in the state. The bandh call given by Assam *Jatiyatabadi Yuba Parishad* just before the election on September, 24 against state terrorism and another statewide ten hour bandh, against 'secret killings'[53] allegedly backed by the state government, was spontaneous and total paralysing the normal life all over the state. All business establishments, banks, and educational institutions remained closed during the bandh period.[54] Past experiences had shown that the indigenous political support base of the regional forces in the *Asomiya* areas was not strong enough to make two regional political parties viable. Efforts in this direction was bound to end in weakening of the regional forces as a whole resulting in political advantage to the Congress(I), the only opposition party in the state with a strong support base. However, this time the AGP seemed to have received some succour from the fact that the All Assam Student Union (AASU), a main stay of *Asomiya* regional sentiments[55] decided not to oppose the poll in sharp contrast to the 1998 elections when the AASU had called a 23 hour bandh to protest against holding of polls as their demand for deletion of the names of foreigners from the electoral rolls was not met. Moreover, the president of the organization, Sarbananda Sonowal relinquished his post and joined AGP to become party's candidate for the Lakhimpur constituency. At the same time a split within the UMF, an ally of Congress, affected the electoral prospect of the Congress. The Hafiz faction of the UMF merged with Nationalist Congress Party (NCP) and another faction led by Osmani merged with the Indian National Congress (INC) before the election. The Jamiat Ulema-e-Hind's decision to support the INC all over the country helped the INC to retain substantial support of the religious minority voters.[56]

The insurgent groups were playing a dominant role in influencing the democratic process in Assam. It is necessary to keep in mind that the ULFA'S role in 1998 polls came under focus following its active campaign against the ruling AGP through coercion, intimidation and even murder of the active workers and district level leaders. This campaign of the banned outfit resulted in the staying away of large segments of the electorate from the battle of ballot in 1998. With the fear psychosis gripping large areas of Brahmaputra valley on account of the grave threat from the banned outfit, the exercise of franchise by the people was severely affected. In the 1999 ULFA did not openly call for the boycott of the election but the Assam Tribune reported that in an issue of its mouth-piece, Swadhinata, it vowed to make this election a bloody one.[57] But the situation in Assam underwent a sea change owing to the assertion of democratic right to vote by a large section of the people. Despite bandh calls and some incidents of violence, like the murder of BJP's candidate from Dhubri, gunning down of three AGP supporters and police personnel, the people participated in the election in large numbers. In Nalbari district for example, which is considered to be a hotbed of insurgent activities, the polling was peaceful and 48 percent voters had exercised their franchise.[58] Voters, including members of ULFA leader families have silently registered their conscious defiance and the threat.

The campaign seemed to be colourless. Confronted by many problems including insurgency, ethnic conflicts and the growing unemployment people seemed to see very little light even in the most vital democratic exercise. As news paper reports show apart from a couple of posters and graffiti put forward by parties like — the Congress, *Asom Gana Parishad* and BJP, no other visible election campaign was witnessed in the state. Election fever was significantly low this time. There were no big rallies, processions or proper campaigning. It appeared that political parties tried to get votes by levelling charges and accusations against each other on the issue of carrying favour with the ULFA for electoral purpose. The euphoria over Kargil issue seemed to be present in some parts of Assam. A CSDS survey showed that in those parts there was a strong swing towards the BJP. The party retained 86 percent of its vote. According to the survey 27 percent of the Congress voters of 1998 shifted to BJP. The BJP made a net gain out of the conflict. Illegal migration of people from the neighbouring Bangladesh was no longer the main poll plank of any of the political parties of the state. The AGP preferred to avoid the issue, apparently for the fear of losing immigrants votes. Their manifesto only said that the foreigners living in the state should be deported as per the provisions of the Assam Accord and the erection of the barbed wire fencing along the international border should be completed soon. Significantly the Congress promised to effectively check illegal infiltration and to establish border trade routes at selected location along the international border. However, the Assam State Committee of the BJP made illegal migration one of its main planks, but the manifesto of the National Democratic Alliance (NDA) remained silent on the issue. The NDA manifesto said that the Alliance would maintain territorial integrity of the North Eastern region and would deal with the security related problems. The Nationalist Congress Party in Assam seemed to have tried to shift focus from such contentious issues. It promised to treat North-East as a special developmental zone. The party appeared to have tried to help BJP so that the Congress could be weakened. The left parties maintained a low profile. The creation of a separate state of Bodoland seemed to be the main election plank of the candidates supported by the ethnic-based parties in the Bodo area like the All Bodo Student's Union and the Bodo People's Action Committee.

Lok-Sabha Elections 1999 Replicating 1998

The Lok Sabha elections in Assam in 1999 was more or less a replica of the 1998 Lok Sabha elections with seemingly minor and yet very significant shift in the power balance. The verdict of the electorate was clearly a reflection of the electorate's disillusionment with the Asom Gana Parishad, the torchbearer of regional politics in the state. The AGP and its allies contested 8 seats but failed to retain even a single seat. It could poll only 13,02 percent of votes. The party suffered a split just before the election. It not only divided the committed regional vote between the AGP and the newly formed parties like Asom Gana Sangram Parishad but also eroded the credibility of a party torn apart by personality clashes.[59]

The Congress seemed to have capitalised on the split in the AGP's vote bank, yet its support base had not significantly increased. Undoubtedly the problems faced by regional politics had kept alive the hopes of the national parties like Congress and BJP. The strength and weaknesses of the Congress and the BJP appeared to be a result of aggregation or dis-aggregations of regional political parties based on various ethnic, cultural and regional issues.

Regionalism as Communitarian Politics

The most significant conclusion that can be drawn from the analysis of the Lok Sabha and assembly elections of the period discussed above is that regionalism was becoming a very important force in Assam politics. But this regionalism need not be defined in terms of the politics of a particular geographical area. As is evident from the political pronouncements of the parties that call themselves regional this term has come to acquire a peculiar meaning in Assam and other states of North-East India to refer to a politics that embraces some interest of particular communities represented by parties of that particular area. But "regional" is always pitted against the "national" or at times the "central" that is perceived as the Indian main stream. The conceptions of the regional and national are therefore contextualised only in a discourse of relative deprivation often couched in cultural terms. But the relative deprivation is not confined to the Centre-State or National-Regional realm. Since the interest of most of the communities are being articulated here by their respective educated elites, relative deprivation is often perceived as deprivation in comparison to those with whom they compete for power in the local or so called regional political sphere. Because of this trend competitive electoral politics is acquiring an increasingly communal turn. This communalism cannot be understood in terms of the context in which the concept is used in Indian politics. In the rest of India communal is defined in terms of divisive politics based on religious differences. For instance, one of the pioneers of study of communalism from the historical perspective, Bipan Chandra says, "Communalism is the belief that because a group of people follow a particular religion they have, as a result, common social, political and economic interests."[60] But here in North East India it is defined in terms of divisive politics of cultural communities often called ethnic groups, nationalities or communities. Community defined in terms of cultural markers seems to be emerging as the most important level of political integration and mobilization. It is this phenomenon that seemed to have brought an end to the one party dominance in the electoral politics of Assam. In this context it is important to note that most of the ethnic communities of contemporary northeast are being organised by their respective educated elites or middle classes by focusing on a possibility of being dominated by what I would call their proximate superiors.[61] The *Asomiya* Middle Class for instance, has been targeting its immediate superior in Assam the Bengali middle class in its entire struggles for protection of *Asomiya* identity and protection of what it calls the Assamese interests. All other communities pursue an ethnic politics of this kind. Electoral politics of Assam needs to be understood in this context.

NOTES AND REFERENCES

1. For description of early British expansion in North East India see, Nirode K. Baruah, *David Scott in North-East India, 1802–1831: A Study in British Paternalism*, Munshiram Manoharlal, New Delhi, 1969.
2. For a discussion on the emergence of the Assamese Middle class that we would now prefer to call the *Asomiya* Middle Class, See Manorama Sharma, *Social and Economic Change in Assam: Middle Class Hegemony*, Ajanta Publication, Delhi, 1990.
3. The term national is being used here in the conventional sense to mean the politics at the Indian level of the Indian state though we ourselves have pointed out in another context the state in India needs to be distinguished from the nation. See, A.K. Baruah, "Nationalism, Regionalism and the Problem of Integration" in *In Search of India's Rennaisance, Vol. II*, Centre for Research in Rural and Industrial Development, Chandigarh, 1992, pp. 385–389.
4. See, A.K. Baruah, 'Assam Election 1996: The Congress Debacle', in Girin Phukan and Adil-ul-Yasi (eds.) *Working of Parliamentary Democracy and Electoral Politics in Northeast India*, South Asian Publishers, New Delhi, 1998, pp. 19–30.
5. The term *'Ana-Asomiya'* refers to all non-Assamese while *'Na-Asomiya'* refers to immigrant Muslim settlers of erstwhile East Pakistan who are assimilated in the Assamese culture.
6. Manorama Sharma, *op. cit.*, pp. 113–39.
7. H.K. Barpujari (ed.), *Political History* of Assam, Vol. 1, Government of Assam (Gauhati, 1977), pp. 164–65. It is of course true that the Bengali residents of the then Assam were also represented in these sessions by their own representatives. Bipan Chandra Pal and Kamini Kumar Chandra were prominent among them. *Loc cit.*
8. Guha 1977: App 6, pp. 343–451.
9. *Ibid.*, Appendix 14A.
10. For a discussion on the growth of this nationality see, A.K. Baruah, 'Middle Class Hegemony and the National Question in Assam' In Milton S. Sangma (ed.) *Essays on North East India*, Indus, New Delhi, 1994, pp. 242–272.

11. For a discussion on the immigrant population see Atul Goswami and Jayanta Kr. Gogoi, 'Migration and Demographic Transformation of Assam 1901–1971' in B.L. Abbi (ed.), *North East Region: Problem and Prospects of Development* (Centre for Research in Rural and Industrial Development, Chandigarh, 1984), pp. 60–80. H.K. Barpujari, *North East India: Problems, Policies and Prospects,* Spectrum Publication, Guwahati, 1998, pp. 33–56.
12. See, Manorama Sharma, *op. cit.*
13. Baruah, 1991.
14. A.K. Baruah *Social Tension in Assam: Middle Class Politics,* Purbanchal Prakash, Gauhati, 1990.
15. Proceedings of the meeting of the Assam Congress Legislative Party, February 28, 1968 cited by K.M. Deka, 'Assam the Challenge of Political Integration and Congress Leadership' in Iqbal Narain (ed.), *State Politics in India,* New Delhi, 1976, p. 43.
16. For the history of this politics see, Shibanikinkar Chaube, Hill Politics in North-East India, Orient Longman, New Delhi, 1973, pp. 107–123.
17. Deka, *op. cit,* pp. 38–43.
18. *Loc. cit.*
19. *Ibid.*, pp. 42–43.
20. For accounts of the influence of this group see B.L. Abbi, *op. cit.*, pp. 56–70.
21. Proceedings of the APCC Executive November 27, 1968 cited by Deka, *op. cit.*, pp. 34–35.
22. A.K. Baruah, 'Assam: Playing Ethnic Politics', *Frontline,* May 17, 1996.
23. See, news reports in *Pratidin,* during February 1996.
24. See, the Manifesto of the *Asom Gana Parishad.*
25. See, Manifesto of the CPI(M).
26. See, CPI, Manifesto.
27. See, Manifesto of the BJP.
28. See, Manifesto of the PDF.
29. See Baruah in *Frontline, op. cit.*
30. See, Resolution the State Convention September 6–7, 1994.
31. Gohain, Hiren (1980): *On the Present Movement in Assam,* Shribhumi Publishing, Calcutta, pp. 18–19.
32. As per 1991 census, the percentage of ST population is 12.12 in Assam and they are mainly concentrated in the areas mentioned in the Table 5.
33. To identify immigrant areas, See M. Bhuyan, 'Population of Assam: An Analytical Synthetic Study with special Treatment of Darrang District', unpublished thesis, Gauhati University, 1971. As per 1991 census, percentage of Muslim population in Dhubri was 70.45, Barpeta 56.07 and Nagaon 47.19.
34. *Ajir Asom,* April 5, 1996; *The Assam Tribune,* April 17, 1996.
35. The Tea-Belt area includes Dibrugarh, Jorhat, Lakhimpur, Tezpur constituencies where major chunk of electorates are from tea garden communities.
36. Sandhya Goswami and Archana Sharma, 'Voting Pattern in 1991 Assam Assembly Election, An Analysis', *Teaching Politics,* Vol. XIX Nos. 3 and 4, pp. 75–84, Sandhya Goswami, 'Some Observations on the Assam Lok Sabha Election 1991', *Gauhati University Journal of Arts,* Vol. XXXVI, 1994.
37. For example at Sualkuchi an Assamese dominated area the turnout of voters in the 22 polling stations was only 5 percent, *The Assam Tribune* February

17, 1998. Similarly, in Jalukbari assembly segment, polling percentage was only 28 percent, see, *The Report on General Election* 1998, Government of Assam.

38. *The Assam Tribune,* April 17, 1996.
39. See, *The Assam Tribune,* November 27, 1997; *The Statesman,* January 26, 1998.
40. A Lesson for AGP, editorial, *The Statesman,* March 10, 1998; *North East Times,* January 4, 1998.
41. *The Assam Tribune,* February 2, 1998.
42. *The Sentinel* (editorial), February 6, 1998; *The Assam Tribune* (editorial), February 15, 1998.
43. *The Assam Tribune,* January 26, 1998.
44. The *Assam Tribune,* February 6, 1998; *Dainik Asom,* February 6, 1998.
45. Anubhav Dutta, "Religious Influence in Assam Politics", *The Assam Tribune* March 4, 1998.
46. These surveys were part of the CSDS' *Lokniti* programme coordinated in North East India by A.K. Baruah. The work in Assam was supervised by Sandhya Goswami and was carried out by a large number of investigators specially trained for the purpose. The data generated was published in National news magazines and news papers and is available for consultation in the CSDS.
47. Goswami, Lok Sabha Election Results in Assam, *op. cit.*
48. *The Assam Tribune,* February 16, 1998.
49. *Ajir Asom,* February 5, 1998; *The Sentinel,* February 6, 1998.
50. *The Assam Tribune,* February 16, 1998.
51. See reports in *The North East Times,* August 1 and 27, 1999; *The Assam Tribune,* August 23, 1999; *Agradoot,* August 12, 1999; *Sadin,* August 24, 1999.
52. *The Assam Tribune,* August 2 and 4, 1999; *The North East Times,* August 27, 1999.
53. During the run up to election a series of kidnapping and murders took place in Assam in which the innocent relations and friends of the ULFA leaders and journalists challenging Government's policy towards extremist politics were the targets. The vernacular press provided clear evidence of the involvement of the state government, surrendered ULFA activists (SULFA) and Army in these murders. These murders came to be known as 'Secret killings in' Assam.
54. *The North East Times,* September 13, 1999 and *Dainik Asom,* Sept. 13, 1999.
55. For information on this organization and the issues raised by it see, Apurba K. Baruah, *Student and Youth Organization in North East India,* Report of an ICSSR, NERC, Project, submitted to ICSSR-NERC, Shillong 2000.
56. *The North East Times,* August 27, 1999.
57. *The Assam Tribune, op. cit.,* August 26, 1999.
58. See, reports in *The Assam Tribune,* August 27, 1999; *Asombani,* August 27, 1999.
59. *The Dainik Asom* (1999), September, 25, Guwahati.
60. Bipan Chandra, *Communalism in Modern India,* Vikash, New Delhi, 1987, p. 1.
61. For a discussion of this process see, Apurba K. Baruah, "Communities and Democracy: A North East Indian Perspective" *North East India Studies,* Vol. I, No. 1, pp. 13–31.

Electoral Politics in Meghalaya: Tribal Loyalties and Interest Articulation

Apurba K. Baruah and *Pascal Malngiang*

In the studies of electoral politics in India the small hill states of India's north-eastern region do not seem to figure prominently. Major publications on politics of elections or electoral politics of the country, these states seem to ignore these small states. But inquiries in to the electoral politics of these states can throw some significant light on the complexities of democratic politics in the country. Such an attempt should help us avoid essentially simplistic conclusions about the electoral politics of the country, governed by the assumption that it is possible to discover an all India pattern despite the socio-political diversities that exist in the country. Such attempts often forget that though the country adopted a political system that tried to bring in some uniformity in the electoral process yet the variations in the value structures of the various politically distinguishable regions shape the nature of electoral politics in remarkably different ways in the respective regions. Therefore, conclusions like that a two party system has emerged as a key feature of party politics in India in the 1990s is the emergence of two party competition, or that the most distinguishing characteristic of elections in the 1990s in India is the increase in party competition measured in terms of *winning differential*. These tribal states reflect a completely different reality of electoral politics in India so far as party competition is concerned.

Among the "Tribal" states of India's North East Meghalaya stands out as one in which competitive politics seems to have taken roots. This competitive politics do not strictly follow the pattern of electoral politics practised in the "mainstream India". Very strong influence of kinship ties and small constituencies enable the political elite to control voting behaviour through personal contacts and influences. As a result ideologies, party affiliations and political programmes do not seem to matter. But the competition for political power often effected through defections, itself is some thing note worthy. Change of government in the state has been so frequent that Governmental instability has become a hallmark of Meghalya politics. But the political significance, or the lack of it, of this competition could be understood only in the context of the electoral history of the state.

Electoral Demography and Background

Meghalaya, originated in the form of an autonomous state, carved out of the composite state of Assam by the Constitution (Twenty second) Amendment Act, 1969. The creation of this autonomous state encouraged a section of the elite, of the tribal communities, of the area covered by it, to believe that most of their grievances would be fulfilled by the new arrangement and hence the enactment was hailed as a Christmas gift for the people of these Hills. The political power in the state was formally transferred in to the hands of a newly emerging western educated tribal elite, that led a virtually peaceful mass movement for its creation, under the leadership of the All Party Hill Leaders' conference. W.A. Sangma, a Garo leader, was sworn in as the chief minister along with four other cabinet ministers, all belonging to the All Party Hill Leaders Conference (APHLC). A smaller party dominated by a section of the Khasis, the Hill State Peoples' Democratic Party (HSPDP) was not in favour of accepting the autonomous state and threatened to agitate. They wanted nothing less than a full-fledged State.[1] A provisional assembly was set up with 38 members elected by an electoral college from the Autonomous District Councils in pursuance of Part VII, Section 62 of the Assam Reorganisation (Meghalaya) Act, 1969. The pressure for a full fledged state continued and on November 10, 1970, full statehood was granted to Meghalaya.[2] From the very beginning the politics of this new state, which was expected to fulfil the expectations of the Khasi-Jaintias and the Garos, unfolded conflicting tribal loyalties that seemed to have generated unprecedented governmental instability. An analysis of the seventh Assembly elections clearly reveals this.

Meghalaya elections for the seventh Assembly, held on 29, February 2003, resulted in a fractured verdict and caused some major upsets because twenty-eight sitting MLAs and two former chief ministers lost. A comparison of the results of Assembly elections of 1998 and 2003 would make one wonder whether the support structures of parties and political equations, in terms of "regional" and "national" allegiance, have undergone radical changes. In 1998, the United Democratic Party (UDP), a regional party with 20 seats, and the Indian National Congress (INC), a national party with 25 seats, were the major players in the post election scenario. Vote share of parties in this election indicates that the national parties comprising the Indian National Congress, the Nationalist Congress Party (NCP), the Bharatiya Janta Party (BJP), and the Communist Party of India (CPI) was 55 percent while the regional parties including the UDP, The Meghalaya Democratic Party (MDP), The Hill State Peoples Democratic Party (HSPDP), The Khun U. Hynniewtrep National Awakening Movement (KHNAM), The Peoples' Democratic Movement (PDM) The Garo National Council (GNC) and the Khasi Farmers Democratic Party (KFDP) could garner only 32.82 percent support. The total vote share of the independent candidates was 12.17 percent.

In 2003 the major players were the two national parties, the INC with 22 seats and the NCP with 14. The largest regional party in the 2003 Assembly, UDP secured only 9 seats, and all other regional parties put together could win only 7 seats. As Table 1 figures show this is the first time that the regional parties were reduced to such a status. Vote share wise too, the regional parties have suffered a set back.

There of course are other interesting developments thrown up by these elections. In an Assembly of sixty members, the INC won twenty-two seats, three seats less than its tally of 25 in 1998. The NCP, a new entrant in Meghalaya electoral politics, captured fourteen seats. BJP which won 3 seats in 1998 and had great dreams of bettering its performance had to be satisfied with only two seats. UDP one of the formidable players in the last assembly won nine seats, a loss of 11. The breakaway group of the UDP, christened as Meghalaya Democratic Party (MDP), could win only four seats. The HSPDP, a regionalist party with strong pro-Khasi sentiments managed two seats, one seat less than in 1998. The KHNAM, a party formed just before the elections by the leaders of the most visible and assertive students union of the state, the Khasi Students Union (KSU), in the same style as the Asom Gana Parishad (AGP) of All Assam Students' Union (AASU), won two seats. This verdict created a situation in the Assembly that threatened to plunge the state into another period of governmental instability and attendant horse-trading. On March 2, the INC as the largest political party in the new Assembly staked claim to form the government with the support of thirty-eight MLAs belonging to the Congress, the UDP, the MDP and three independents. The NCP was quick to stake a counter claim but without specifying the sources of its support. The Governor went by the principle of inviting the largest party in the Assembly to form the Government. Eventually a new alliance called Meghalaya Democratic Alliance (MDA) was formed with 42 MLAs (INC 22, UDP 9, MDP 4 HSPDP 2, KHNAM 2 and independents 3).[3] Of these 42 MLAs, 38 were inducted into the cabinet. The leader of the second largest party in the coalition belonging to the UDP, Donkupar Roy, was appointed the deputy chief minister after the UDP MLAs expressed unhappiness over the distribution of portfolios and the NCP floated an idea of an alternative government with Donkupar Roy as the Chief minister.[4] The jumbo cabinet, of course, was an obvious attempt by the coalition to foil any attempt at defection, indicating the possibilities of instability. NCP's move at winning away some coalition partners too clearly indicated possibilities of horse-trading and governmental instability which had become the hall marks of Meghalaya politics.

Ever since the state was carved out of the composite state of Assam, in 1972, unstable coalitions and governmental instability have been the rules rather than the exceptions in the electoral politics of this hill state. Barring the first elections, the electorate had never given a clear verdict (Table 1). In the Assembly elections of 1972, of the 60 seats in the house, the All Party Hill Leaders' Conference (APHLC) won 39 seats, the Congress and the Hill State People's Democratic Party (HSPDP) won 12, and 8 seats respectively. In those elections only one independent candidate could win. Thus, the verdict was clear and the regional parties together won 47 seats in the 60 member Assembly. But this clear verdict and the resultant stability did not last. In 1976 the APHLC split under the pressures of national politics of the early period of the emergency declared by Indira Gandhi.[5] On November 22, a Congress ministry was installed as a result of the split in the APHLC, and a politics of defections, unstable coalitions and repeated fractured verdicts in elections began.

The developments of 1976, however, did not prove that the support base of the regional politics was fragile because except for the 2003 elections, the National parties could never win a majority of seats in the Assembly. A look at the performance of the national and regional parties in the state elections over the years shows clearly that Meghalaya politics remain dominated by regional forces. Except for the elections of 2003 in all the Assembly elections held after the creation of the state the votes polled by the regional parties together have been much more than the votes polled by the national parties (Table 5).

Despite such hold over the electorate the regional political parties have not been able to govern the state without sharing power with the "national" parties because the regional parties suffered from repeated splits and frequent defections and as a result National parties could play significant roles in exercise of political power. So far as the question of sharing of power among themselves is concerned, most of the regional parties seem to exhibit a glaring incompatibility with other regional parties. This incompatibility reflects an ideological inconsistency because the particular regional forces seem to find themselves more comfortable in coalitions with national parties rather than in alliances with other regional parties of the state. These peculiarities of electoral politics of the state cannot be understood without looking at the history of the state.

Historical Background

The 1972 elections in the state were held in the aftermath of a more or less peaceful popular movement leading to the formation of a separate state for the tribal people of the Khasi, Jaintia and Garo hills of the erstwhile composite state of Assam.[6] Though many politicians and opinion builders have been arguing that the main cause of the demand for re-organization of the composite state of Assam was Assamese linguistic chauvinism, reflected in the insistence of the *Asomiya* community on adopting Assamese as the official language, yet we have argued elsewhere that the demands for homelands, political autonomy and separate states made by various communities of the British created composite state of Assam had deeper reasons like emergence of new social forces in the smaller communities of the region.[7] The movement for creation of a separate state for hill people was led by the newly emerging educated elite of the Khasi-Jaintia[8] and the Garo communities. Among these tribal communities, formidable social forces like feudal lords, or bourgeoisie are absent and the working population is unorganised. Sushmita Sengupta has shown that in Meghalaya, even in the nineties of the last century, clan relations were strong because class relations had not yet been able to replace those and that in the absence of industrialization the proletariat also had not emerged as a class.[9] The level of stratification in most areas is still low. This is not surprising because at the time of the coming of the British to the area in the nineteenth century, except for the *Jaintia* ruled by a King, other peoples lived under some traditional chiefs, leading small communities that practiced shifting cultivation[10] and adhered to tribal communitarian practices. The British did not interfere much with their social life except for introducing Christianity and western education. As a result of introduction of western education during the British rule small educated-elite have emerged in the tribal communities.[11] Implementation of policies under protective discrimination later by the Indian State helped this elite strengthen their position in their respective communities and over the years they acquired intellectual and moral leadership in their respective communities.[12] Acquisition of some wealth by siphoning off development funds further helped them consolidate their position. This development has not brought about significant changes in the political value premises of the large majority of the people concerned because guarantees under the Sixth Schedule[13] encouraged the continuation of some of the tribal practices and values through the traditional political institutions, at least among the masses. These practices and values are being used by some sections of the elite to significant political advantage. Therefore, adaptation of these communities to the democratic values, attached to the system of governance established by the Constitution of India, is still strenuous.[14] As a result kinship ties and tribal loyalties often override the ideological or party loyalties and at times even individual interests. But the scenario as we shall see is fast changing.

Tribal Loyalties and Elections

The three major tribes of the state, the Khasis, the Jaintias and the Garos live in clearly demarcated areas: the Khasi Hills, the Jaintia Hills and the Garo Hills. In the absence of major social forces capable of ideologically mobilizing the populace, the election results could be expected to reflect the preferences of the respective tribes in their own areas. If we go by the theory of kinship loyalties overriding other political considerations in relatively less developed societies, the *Khasi-Jaintia* can be expected to reflect a commonality in their electoral preferences because this group claims to belong to one cultural tradition. **In this context we need to point out that clan divisions within each of these small tribes do not affect electoral politics because most of the clans are too small in size and the relatively bigger ones are no longer living together. Other factors that erode the influence of clans are the larger identity of tribe, now often called nationality by tribal leaders, and the influence of the Christian organizations.**

The "tribal" or nationality identity and religious identity claim supra-clan loyalties. For instance the Khasi educated elite is now making political capital out of an origin myth called Hynniewtrep. So much so, that the Khasi Students Union has christened its newly formed political party as Khun Hynniewtrep National Awakening Movement (KHNAM). According to this myth, in the beginning of time, God created nine families or, *Khathynriew trep Khathynriew Skum*. They remained with God in heaven. Later on by a covenant, seven of those came down to earth. They had free access to heaven through the Golden ladder (*Ka jingkieng ksiar*) believed to be located at *Lum Sohpet bneng* or the Navel of Heaven Hill situated in the northern part of Shillong. Man's pride and sins, led to the breaking down of the ladder. Therefore, these seven families, believed to be the ancestors of the Khasis were known as *Ki Hynniewtrep ki Hynniew skum* or the Seven huts, the Seven families. The authors of the late 19th and the beginning of the 20th century did not use the term Hynniewtrep frequently. It surfaced only in the book of Rabon Singh, *Ka Kitab Niam Khein ki Khasi* in the year 1904. He wrote that "The Hynniewtrep Hynniew skum are seven pairs of people, females and males, that God created...From these, people spread to different parts of the Khasi and Jaintia Hills. The term Hynniewtrep came to the limelight with writings of the renowned Khasi poet, u Soso Tham. He christened his book *Ki Sngi barim u Hynniewtrep* or the Olden days of the Hynniewtreps. Verses from this poem are now cited frequently at various circles. However, the term gained currency only in the late 1970s in the wake of the students' agitations against the influx of foreigners into the state. Immediately after the anti-Bangladeshi stir of the 1978–79, the Hynniewtrep National Front, a political party was formed. In its second anniversary held at Shillong on November 25, 1981, it demanded a separate Hynniewtrep State comprising the Khasi and Jaintia Hills. It claimed that the need for the reorganisation of the State was felt to be a necessity for the sake of development and not due to any enmity with the Garos. This demand was later taken up by the HSPDP. In other areas too the term gained momentum with social organisations using it. For instance, the Hynniewtrep Cultural and Welfare Organisation (HTCWO) was formed in the late 70s and the Hynniewtrep Endeavour Society (HES) formed on April 10, 1989. Influential Khasi scholars and writers who popularised this term were Donbok T. Laloo, L. Gilbert Shullai and Fr. Sylvanus Sngi Lyngdoh. These authors frequently used this term in their popular writings when referring to the Khasis and the Pnars. If the term was used politically from the late 70s it would not be wrong to suggest that the new political scenario that emerged after the creation of the state of Meghalaya had some thing to do with its political importance. Till the formation of the state the Khasi, Jaintia and Garo elites viewed the *Asomiya Middle Class* as their main political competitor. Therefore they closed ranks. But the number game in the new state necessitated mobilization of the three tribal communities on their respective ethnic lines, particularly because within the state itself each of these communities had their perceived "home lands" of their own. When KHNAM adopted its name after many consultations with its past and present members it was clear that the term Hynniewtrep was being used by the Khasis as an instrument of ethnic mobilization. The use of the term Hynniewtrep is often claimed to be primarily meant to emphasise the bonds of unity among the Khasis and the Pnars and to do away with the feelings that the two communities are different. The myth seems to do this by claiming a common origin. But the implications of linguistic differences between the Khasis and Jaintias are a little too important particularly in view of the hegemonic position enjoyed by the educated elites in their respective communities, to be obliterated by discovery or invention of common origin myths. It is necessary to note that even though the Jaintia Students Union (JSU) initially agreed to join hands with the KSU to form a political party but later it withdrew leaving the KSU alone to launch KHANM. Similar efforts at ethnic mobilization is under way among the Garos around the concept of *Achik Mamde*. It is natural that with the emergence of consciousness about larger identities like that of the Hynniewtrep, clan identity would come to play only a small role in politics, particularly in electoral politics, in which numerical strength becomes a crucial factor.

As the Table 3 indicates, the Garo areas, comprising the districts of South Garo Hills, East Garo Hills and West Garo Hills, seemed to be strong holds of National political parties during the period from 1972 to 1988. Of the seven Assembly elections held during this period only in two, i.e. in 1972 and 1988, the regional parties could win fifty percent or more seats. The performance of regional parties seems to have suffered a sharp decline in these areas from 1990s. In 1993, 1998 and 2003 elections the regional parties could win only 2, 3 and 2 seats respectively out of 24. This is in sharp contrast to the performance of the regional forces in 1972. In that election, the APHLC won 17 seats out of the 24 in the area. The INC won 5 and 2 seats went to independents. Williamson A. Sangma, a Garo leader became the chief minister of the state. Later on it was he himself who took the lead to split the APHLC in 1976 and to merge with the Congress. This move was bitterly opposed to by most of the senior Khasi leaders of the APHLC.[15] **From then on till 2003 the differences between the Garo and the Khasi-Jaintia areas also appeared to be on national and regional lines, the former preferring the national, and the latter, more often than not, supporting the regional forces.** The reasons behind this need not necessarily be sought in factional politics or personality clashes, though during the last elections local analysts were trying to explain the results in terms of Purno A. Sangma's machinations against his Garo rivals in and outside the Congress. **The North Eastern experience of democratic mobilization clearly suggests, that when the educated elite or the educate middle class of a less developed community begins to emerge it tries to benefit by remaining close to more powerful and hegemonic forces. But when it gains strength it uses regional or ethnic politics as a bargaining strategy.**[16]

For instance, the nascent Assamese educated elite of the nineteenth century towed the British line and even tried to follow the more advanced Bengali elite but once it gained strength it began a politics of anti-British Indian nationalism and eventually moved to aggressive Assamese nationalism.[17] Things were not different in the case of the Khasi and the Garo elites. So far as western education is concerned the Khasi-Jaintias have an advantage. During the British period itself Shillong, in East Khasi Hills district, became a centre of quality schools and colleges. Quantity wise too, in the state Khasi Hills have the largest concentration of educational institutions of higher level. With the establishment of the North Eastern Hill University (NEHU) in Shillong after the creation of the state of Meghalaya, the numerical strength of the Khasi-Jaintia educated sections grew impressively. Even the discrepancy in literacy rates of the Garo and Khasi-Jaintia areas shows this clearly. According to the 2001 census the Khasi-Jaintia areas have a literacy rate of 66.6 percent while the Garo areas remain at 55.85. Going by the Census of India, the Khasi-Jaintia Graduates both in the urban and rural areas outnumber their Garo counter parts in the two previous censuses. The figures in Table 6 indicates our above contention. If we apply the theory of the size of the educated elite or the middle class being directly related to the decline of support for more powerful and hegemonic forces and the use of regional or ethnic politics as a bargaining strategy being directly related to its gaining of strength then it would appear to be only natural that the Garo political elite would continue to align with national parties and that the Khasi elite would encourage the regional parties.

There is no doubt that the *Khasi-Jaintia* educated elite understands that one of the ways of capturing resources of the state is by mobilizing people on ethnic lines to influence the number game of democratic politics. The *Khasi-Jaintia* ethnic politics seemed to have become more and more strident over the years, particularly, from the mid eighties. This is clearly reflected in the aggressive ethnic politics of the students and youth organizations[18] leading to large-scale disturbances in the urban areas.[19] The aggressive ethnocentric politics of the *Khasi-Jaintia* educated elite strengthens the regional parties in the area but at the same time the shrill *Khasi* nationalism alienates the relatively weaker Garo educated elite. In the 1960s and 70s, the Garo educated elite was a partner in the tribal assertions in the region. Many educated Garos were leaders of the APHLC, the party that led the Hill State movement. Garo National Conference supported the movement.[20] But by 1990s the alienation was such that the organizations like the Garo National Council and the aggressive sections of the *Khasi* educated elite were in two different poles of politics on issues like reservation of jobs, shifting of head quarters of the Meghalaya Board of Secondary Education.[21] As a result the Garo electorate seems to be turning away from the regional parties dominated by Khasis. **Garo educated elite is still in its formative stage and is yet to find it necessary and opportune to come out of the umbrella of national political forces and to vigorously pursue a regional politics based Garo identity.** That is why elections in Garo Hills, as distinct from the Khasi Hills, remain dominated by the National parties. In the last elections as many as 19 seats, out of the 24 in the region, were captured by the national parties (Table 3). But in view of the facts that the regional parties in Meghalaya are Khasi dominated and the Garo elite distancing itself from these parties and remaining with the national parties, the regional national divide in Meghalaya politics is increasingly becoming a tribal divide.

The poor performance of the regional parties in the last election needs to be understood also in the context of the gradual but steady decline of these parties in Meghalaya ever since the 1976 split in the APHLC. As Table 1 shows these parties never actually recovered from that split. One of the reasons for the split in the dark days of emergency was that, without merging with the Congress (I) the leadership in power would not have survived. This pursuit for power by the various sections of the elite led to repeated splits in regional parties and also to the emergence of new parties. That the splits and the emergence of new regional parties strengthen national parties in electoral battle became clear in the 2003 elections too. As we have noted in the 1998 Assembly, the UDP was one of the major parties with 20 seats. But internal squabbles led to a split in the party and a break-away section contested the 2003 elections under the banner of the MDP. The Meghalaya United Democratic Party (MUDP) which was later renamed as MDP at the First Convention of the Party was formed by a group of eight MLAs belonging to the UDP. They demanded that the Chief Minister who was allegedly involved in the Kolkata Meghalaya House scam deal, should resign. However, the Chief Minister did not do so despite popular protests taking place against him. Several social organisations like the Khasi Students Union (KSU), the Federation of Khasi Jaintia and Garo People (FKJGP), the Synjuk Seng Samla Shnong, The Synjuk ki Rangbah Shnong (an association of Headmen), The Shillong We Care, the Jaintia Students Union, and the Khasi Women's Welfare and Development Association (KWWADA) met together at a rally called Peoples' Rally Against Corruption (PRAC) and demanded that he should step down. In view of this pressure on the Government, the eight MLAs resigned from the cabinet and formed the MUDP. This split led to a splitting of the support base of the regional parties, particularly, the UDP. The decision of the Khasi Students Union (KSU) to form KHNAM also seemed to have seriously affected the performance of UDP and thus helped INC perform better in Khasi Hills. As the Table 4 shows, in as many as 11 constituencies the MDP and KHNAM either facilitated the INC by splitting the regional vote base or reduced the margin of defeat of the INC. In six of these constituencies won by INC, UDP+MDP or UDP+KHNAM votes would have surpassed the votes polled by INC. Since UDP, MDP and KHNAM appealed to the voters on the same *Khasi* community plank it is reasonable to conclude that by contesting in the same constituencies they helped INC by dividing the anti-INC votes of the Khasi people. The only constituency where KHNAM seems to have seriously jeopardised the prospects of INC was Jaiaw. But Jaiaw tells a different story too.

Opportunity vs Ideology: The Jaiaw Syndrome

An analysis of election results would also show that the political class in contemporary Meghalaya at times rises above ethnic loyalties in pursuit of personal interests though when it suits them they would pursue ethnic politics. It is not surprising to find ethnocentric regional political forces changing their colours swiftly to join mainstream nationalist forces or *vice-versa*. A look at the electoral politics of the prestigious Jaiaw constituency, in Shillong, during 1998 and 2003 Assembly elections reveals this clearly. In the 1998 Martamlin Pyrbot contested from the Jaiaw constituency of Shillong, the capital city of Meghalaya in a right wing nationalist party (BJP) ticket and secured 2381 votes. The INC candidate secured 1397 votes bringing the tally of the national parties to 3778 votes in a constituency of 9966 votes. The UDP candidate A.H. Scott Lyngdoh, a cabinet minister in the last government winner of two previous elections, won the seat with 4430 votes. An independent candidate polled 1499 votes and 259 votes were rejected. The difference between the votes polled by the regional parties and the national parties were only 652. In 2003, four regional parties namely, HSPDP, UDP, MDP (a break away section of UDP) and KHNAM contested. Paul Lyngdoh a former president of the Khasi Student Union, won as the KHNAM candidate with 5873 votes. Among themselves the regional parties now captured 11739 votes. Martamlin Pyrbot turned completely around from the right wing nationalist politics of BJP, contested from HSPDP, a hard core Khasi regionalist party, and polled 2283 votes. INC the only national party to contest from this constituency in 2003 polled only 519 votes. Scott Lyngdoh, the 1998 winner, broke away from UDP and contested from the newly formed MDP and polled 1347 votes. The INC suffered because it fielded an unknown personality. Its candidate in 1998, Maya R. Kyndiah now contested from the regionalist UDP and polled only 234 votes. The result was perplexing. On the one hand, in 1998 two national parties (BJP and INC) contested and together they polled 3778 votes and in 2003 only one national party INC was contesting and therefore the INC should have been able at least to retain a large number of votes it polled in 1998. But its vote share depleted surprisingly to 519. On the other hand, the 4 regional parties contesting in 2003 in the constituency should have been expected to divide the regional votes polled by the only regional party that contested in 1998, the UDP, and therefore the national party candidate should have won. But such assessments are totally misplaced in Meghalaya because the politicians have no hesitation in shifting from regional to national parties and *vice versa* and the electorate seems to follow individual candidates and not parties. The only thing that matters is power. A post election development made the point tellingly. The victorious candidate from Jaiaw fought from a hard core ethnocentric position and emerged as one of the strongest critics of mainstream Indian politics. He demanded greater share of reservations in government jobs for the Hynniewtrep people than the Garos and, in the run up to the elections, raised demands for the removal of Army head quarters from Shillong on the plea that Army's presence might invite enemy attacks endangering the Hynniewtrep people. After the elections he joined the Government led by INC. All ethnic and regional sentiments were put aside on the plea that the INC led Government had parties from the Hynniewtrep and therefore it was legitimate to participate in that. Pursuit of power as ideology weighs heavily in Meghalaya politics, particularly among the educated elite and their organizations. Jaiaw is not an exception it is a typical Meghalaya constituency.

The results of 2003 Assembly elections confirm the conclusion that national issues or ideological considerations are of little importance in Meghalaya politics. Precisely because of this the election manifestoes do not matter here. A perusal of the 2003 manifestoes showed that all the parties were making the right noises. KHNAM was different because it had a sophisticatedly written manifesto but the message was the same — we need honest government who can protect the cultural identity of the people and maintain stability and achieve development. Well, the stage was set long time back in 70s when the APHLC called itself a regional party with a national out look and the Congress called itself a national party with a regional out look. A nice and mouth watering *Khichuri* for the voters.

Table 1: Meghalaya Legislative Assembly: Party wise Break Up of Seats Won from 1972 to 2003

Year	National Parties				Regional Parties														IND	Total
	INC	NCP	BJP	CPI	AHL	HPD	PDC	MP-PP	APH-LC	APH-LC(a)	UDP	MDP	GNC	HSP-DP	KHN-AM	PDM	PDIC	HPU		
72	9			0	0	0	0		32					8			0		11	60
78	20			0	0	0	0		16					14			2		8	60
83	25			0	15	15	2		0					0			0		3	60
88	22			0						2				6			2	19	9	60
93	24		0	0				2		3				8			2	11	10	60
98	25	0	3	0							20	0	1	3	0	3			5	60
03	22	14	2	0							9	4	0	2	2	0			5	60

Source: Calculated from the Meghalaya Election Department Figures.

Table 2: Vote Share of Political Parties in the 2003 Elections

Name of Parties	Jaintia Hills	Khasi Hills*	Garo Hills**
INC	35.22	29.45	28.59
NCP	15	7.01	34.5
BJP	1.36	6.09	6.21
SP	–	0.2	0.06
UDP	31.14	18.29	7.87
MDP	6.54	9.62	0.16
HSPDP	3.86	9.85	–
PDM	.26	2.79	1.3
GNC	–	–	2.31
KHNAM	.17	8.15	–
KFDP	–	0.62	–
IND	6.42	7.86	18.97

Source: Calculated from the Meghalaya Election Handbook 2003.

* Khasi hills include the East and West Khasi Hills and Ri Bhoi districts.

** Garo Hills has three districts.

Table 3: Performance of Regional and National Parties in Elections During 1972–2003 Regional Break-Up of Garo and Khasi-Jaintia Areas

Year	Garo				Khasi-Jaintia			
	Regional	National	Ind	Total	Regional	National	Ind	Total
1972	17	05	2	24	23	4	9	36
1978	08	11	5	24	24	9	3	36
1983	05	18	1	24	27	7	2	36
1988	12	07	5	24	17	15	4	36
1993	02	14	8	24	24	10	2	36
1998	03	18	3	24	24	10	2	36
2003	02	19	3	24	15	19	2	36

Source: Calculated from Meghalaya Election Department Figures.

Table 4: Splits and Electoral Performance of Regional Parties in 2003

Constituency	INC	UDP	MDP	KHNAM	Difference between 1 and 2+3+4=RS/RD*
1. Mawhati	5201	4270	–	1082	151 (RS)
2. Nongpoh	7808	6100	–	670	1038 (RD)
3. Jirang	2888	2687	–	458	743 (RD)
4. Mairang	5594	2847	4549	360	1162 (RS)
5. Sohiong	9518	7209	–	695	1614 (RD)
6. Malki-Nongthymmai	5384	2792	66	1700	826 (RD)
7. Sohrinkham	4388	1612	3530	–	754 (RS)
8. Lyngkerdem	2832	1602	2415	591	1776 (RS)
9. Nongskhen	4235	1783	–	3182	730 (RS)
10. Pariong	4427	4398	–	1157	1128 (RS)
11. Langrin	4460	3514	–	835	1142 (RD)

Source: Calculated from Meghalaya Election Department data.

* RS stands for excess of UDP+MDP+KHNAM votes over votes polled by INC in the constituencies won by INC. RD stands for deficit of the UDP+MDP+KHNAM votes in terms of votes polled by INC.

Table 5: Valid Votes Polled by Parties and Percentage thereof

Year	National Parties	Regional Parties	Independents
1972	10.5	35.5*	54
1978	31.02	44.16	24.82
1983	22.49	61.91	15.57
1988	33.01	47.39	19.58
1993	38.89	44.07	17.02
1998	38.5	44.53	16.96
2003	55	32.83	12.17

Source: Calculated from the Meghalaya Election Handbooks, Election Department.

* Three candidates of the Regional parties were declared elected uncontested.

Table 6: Number of Graduates among Garos and Khasis

Community	1981	1991	Total
Garo	594	1310	1904
Khasis	4526	10135	14661

Source: Census of India of the relevant years.

NOTES AND REFERENCES

1. *Ibid.*, April, 2, 1970.
2. *Ibid.*, March 15, 1969.
3. *Ibid.*, November 14, 1970. 3 See, *The Shillong Times*, March 3, 4, and 5, 2003.
4. See, *The Shillong Times*, March 7, 2003.
5. S.K. Chaube, *Electoral Politics In North-East India* (Sangam Books, Calcutta, 1985) and Sushmita Sengupta, *Regionalism in Meghalaya* (unpublished Ph.D. thesis, North Eastern Hill University, Shillong, 1997) discuss the emergence and development of regional forces in some details.
6. For a discussion of the movement and the history of the hill politics in India's north-east see, Shibanikinkar Chaube, *Hill Politics In North-East India* (Orient Longman, Calcutta, 1973). See, A.K. Baruah, "Reorganization of Composite State of Assam and Linguistic Chauvinism of Asomiyas" *Proceedings of North East India History Association*, Seventeenth Session, Aizawl, 1997, pp. 292–296.
7. A.K. Baruah, "Reorganization of Composite Assam and the Linguistic Chauvinism of the Asomiyas", *Proceedings of the North East India History Association*, Seventeenth Session, Aizawl, 1997, pp. 292–296.
8. Though the Khasis and the Jaintias inhabit two distinct hilly areas in the Khasi hills and the Jaintia hills yet most of the Khasi and Jaintia scholars insist that these two communities belong to the same cultural tradition. Jaintias are also called the Syntegs or the people left behind. For a history of the Khasi-Jaintias, see, Namita Cathrine Shadap-Sen, *The Origin and Early History of the Khasi-Synteng People* (Firma KLM, Calcutta, 1981).
9. Sushmita Sengupta, Communist Party of India in Meghalaya, unpublished M.Phil thesis, North Eastern Hill University, Shillong, 1988, p. 158.
10. *Khasi* Chiefs were known as *Syiems* and the areas ruled by them were called *Syiemships*. Historians and British official records refer to 25 such Syiemships, variously identified as Republics and Oligarchies. For a discussion see, Manorama Sharma, "Critiquing Traditions: The Case of Meghalaya", paper presented in an *International Workshop on Community, Conflicts and Crisis of Democratic Governance: An Analysis of the Societies of North East India*, held in North Eastern Hill University, Shillong, 18–19 September, 2002. The *Garos* had their own traditional systems under Nokmas. For discussions on some of these systems see, Jayanta Sarkar and B. Datta Ray, *Social and Political Institutions of the Hill People of North East India* (Anthropological Survey of India, Calcutta, 1990).
11. For some indications of emergence of this elite in Meghalaya see, Ashish Bose *et al.* (eds.) *Tribal Develpoment and Demography in North-East India* (B.R. Publishing, Delhi, 1990).
12. This point was argued by us in some detail in the context of the student movements in North East India. See, Apurba K. Baruah, (ed.) *Student Power in North East India*, Regency Publications, New Delhi, 2002.
13. For a discussion on the Sixth Schedule see, B.L. Hansaria, *Sixth Schedule to the Constitution of India — A Study*, Gita Hansaria, Gauhati, 1983.
14. Apurba K. Baruah, "Tribal Traditions and Crises of Governance in North East India With Special Reference to Meghalaya" *Crisis States Working Papers*, Working Paper No. 22 (www.crisisstates.com).
15. Chaube, *Electoral Politics, op. cit.*, p. 22.

16. See, Apurba Baruah, "Middle Class Hegemony and the National Question in Assam" in Milton Sangma (ed.) *Essays on The North-East India,* (Inter India, Delhi, 1994.) pp.
17. See Apurba K. Baruah, *Social Tensions in Assam: Middle Class Politics* (Purbanchal, Guwahati, 1991).
18. See, Pascal Malngiang, "Students and Youth Organizations in Meghalaya" in Baruah, *Student Power, op. cit.,* pp. 173–196.
19. For evidence of this in the case of Shillong city see, Rakhal K. Purkayastha "Social Instability in Shillong, 1980–1991" in B. Datta Ray (ed.) *Dynamics of a Tribal Society,* Uppal, New Delhi, 1993, pp. 267–284.
20. Chaube, Hill Politics, *op. cit.,* pp. 46–124.
21. In a state with very little private capital and industrialization reservation of government jobs is a major political issue. The KSU has been trying to secure 90 percent job reservation for tribals of the state and of that 50 percent for the Khasis to the great consternation of the Garo youth. The Secondary education board head quarters are in Tura of Garo Hills. The KSU wants it shifted to Shillong. That would give Khasis more control over the jobs in the board.

Ethnic Self-Determination and Electoral Politics in Nagaland

*Rajesh Dev**

The state of Nagaland, known for the oldest insurgent movement in India than any other event has a distinct electoral history. Beginning with the boycott of the first general elections in 1952;[1] the subsequent establishment of an "Interim Council' where members were to be elected according to rules made 'with regard to the custom and usages' of the tribes;[2] the uncontested election of three members from the Naga Hills district of Assam to the Assam Legislative Assembly in 1957[3] and finally the formation of the state of Nagaland in 1963 and elections to the state assembly in 1964, modern representative politics in Nagaland has undergone influential transformation to be affected by the methods and values of liberal democracy.

Though the contestations between the Government of India and the forces — formidably represented by the Naga Insurgents — opposed to the extension of any constitutional authority of the Indian State and the 'forcible integration' of Naga-inhabited areas into India, continued, the interstices of peace ushered by the activities of numerous organisations and individuals[4] nurtured the development of a restricted political space upon which democratic politics was to be consolidated.

It is, however, the formation of the state of Nagaland[5] as the 16th state of the Union of India that is considered by a section of the Naga society as a limited but significant step towards

* An earlier version of this paper was published in the *Economic & Political Weekly*, Vol. 38, No. 17, April 26, 2003.

self-rule. Scholars also accepted the fact that it was only after the first elections to the assembly that "the state government has emerged as a strong institution with a renewed mandate from the people".[6] The Assembly elections necessitated by the formation of the state had as such propelled popular participation in the electoral process. In fact some are more emphatic about the assertion that the gradual marginalisation of the forces opposed to any political links of the Nagas with the union of India began with the first successful elections in Nagaland in 1964.[7] As a consequence elections "as an institutional phenomenon of politics" and democratic mechanism for expressing political preferences and dissent furnished a 'contested legitimacy'[8] to the new state and its structures. The legitimacy is contested because a major portion of the electorate did not initially participate in exercising their franchise[9] thereafter free and fair elections[10] were marred by accusations of severe malpractices. Moreover a neutral and legitimate execution of the electoral process has been undermined by the presence and dominance of the Naga insurgents who exert substantial influence not only on the electoral outcomes but on the dominant issues as well.[11]

However, in order to put electoral politics in Nagaland in perspective it is very important for us to actually elaborate the background in which elections are held in the state that has seen decades of confrontation between state actors and non-state actors each seeking to consolidate its legitimacy as the genuine representative of the 'Naga people'.

The underground, 'Federal Government of Nagaland' formed on the 14th of August 1947 has always maintained through its political wing, the Naga National Council, (NNC) that the Nagas constitute an independent nation[12] and therefore any interference through the establishment of institutions and structures of administration by the Government of India is an extension of the interference in the internal affairs of the Nagas. In order to justify and accord legitimacy to their distinct political claims the NNC supposedly held a Plebiscite in May 1951 where it was claimed that 99.9% of the Nagas expressed the desire and support for independence. Nonetheless, the government of India considered intervention in the "Naga Hills" legitimate by virtue of its 'colonial heritage' that was further vindicated by the Extra-Provincial Jurisdiction Act passed by the British Parliament, which empowered the new Indian Government to continue its administration in the Naga Hills.[13] The evolving discontent of the 'Naga people' were thus expressed initially through the boycott of the first general elections in 1952, when they felt that participation in the electoral process would mean legitimising the structures and institutional processes that the Indian state was extending to a people over whom they had no claim.[14] However, the malleable political intransigence of the Nagas slowly transformed itself into armed insurrection and in 1954 violence erupted in the districts of Tuensang, Kohima and Mokukchoung. These violent assertions of the Nagas were counteracted by the Indian State through the extension of numerous administrative and legal regulations that sought to integrate the Nagas with India and establish the legal juridical supremacy of the Indian state.[15]

The emerging political tryst between the contesting forces fractured political opinions within the Naga society itself and by 1956, the Naga National Movement had openly split into moderate and extremist factions[16] and this resulted in the intensification of violence and tension in the Naga society. The subsequent formation of the First Naga Peoples' Convention in 1957, convened by the moderate sections of the Nagas resolved that (a) the political future of the Naga People lay within the Union of India[17] along with numerous other resolutions. The government of India simultaneously also continued in its efforts to politically engage the Nagas and persuade them to participate in electing representatives to state structures. As a result in 1957 three candidates fought elections from the three constituencies of the Naga Hills to the Assam legislative Assembly, where one of them even became a minister.[18] These efforts of the moderate Nagas continued with increasing attempts to mobilise public opinion against violence and emphasise upon a negotiated settlement to the Naga claims. The Third convention of the Naga People held in 1959 passed a 16-point proposal that was to form the basis of the agreement between the moderate Nagas and the Government of India that recognised that the political goal for the Naga people was a full-fledged state within the union of India.[19] Thus the government of India through the 13th amendment to the constitution moved a bill for the creation of a full-fledged state of Nagaland vide the State of Nagaland Act 1962, finally leading to the inauguration of the state of Nagaland by the President of India in December 1963. Many scholars observe that among the Naga intelligentsia there is a growing realisation that the 16-Point Agreement was a major step in safeguarding the wishes of the Naga people although questions of sovereignty and territoriality were not covered.[20] Nonetheless it is worthwhile to mention that though the 16-Point Agreement formed the basis of the formation of the new state, during the Legislative Assembly elections of February 2003 the contested political significance of the Agreement had become a major political issue among various forces of the Naga Society. Sections of the Naga social and political leadership espousing sympathy for the 'Naga National Cause' declined to accept the Agreement as a final settlement of the 'Indo-Naga' problem and considered it a stop-gap arrangement pending final political settlement.[21]

Notwithstanding these brief periods of co-operation between the government and the moderate sections of the Nagas there had been an increase in the subversive activities of the extremist sections followed by the killings of moderate Naga leaders like Sakhrie, who decided to break away from Phizo's NNC, by the extremist sections. This not only helped to reinforce inter-tribal rivalry among the Nagas but resulted in a situation where "politics seemed no longer to be in command"[22] of the Naga National struggle.

The phenomenon of splits within the Naga movement between those who supported negotiated autonomy and those who sought complete independence also led to the emergence of a paradoxical situation in the new state where claims to legitimacy were shared by 'legally constituted' representatives elected by the people to state structures and the 'ideologically constituted' non-state representatives who superintended the structures of the underground elements but nonetheless exerted extensive influence over the legally constituted state structures. Both the groups continued to draw upon the resources of each other to legitimise their 'representation', hence while the 'legally-constituted' representatives derive ideological resources from the underground elements by maintaining that the present state is merely a stop-gap arrangement, pending a "final solution"; the latter on their part utilise the structures of the state to divert funds and other forms of support for the movement from "sympathizers"[23] in the state structures. This symbiotic relationship[24] between the 'ideological and legal' forces was strengthened during the 1969 elections to the Legislative Assembly when the Democratic Party of Nagaland perceived by many scholars[25] as being considerably influenced by the 'underground elements' became a major player in Nagaland politics. This relationship has today become an accepted feature of Nagaland to the extent that the "underground faction" collects regular revenue through the imposition of 'taxes' on all officials of the "legal faction" including the police personnel and utilise the support services offered by constitutionally legitimated ministers in the state government.[26] In fact this issue has also become adequately blended with electoral politics in the state and as such we find that the regional parties in the state echo a soft sympathy for the insurgents while the national parties either extend a silent indifference to the issue or call for the initiation of a process of dialogue for a resolution.

The resulting 'legitimation dilemma' that evolved in the Naga society and polity continue to bedevil the Nagas even today when calls for a reconciliation between various groups claiming to represent the Naga people fail to arrive at any consensual conciliation primarily due to the fact that the society and polity is fractured not only by its myriad tribal loyalties but also by its support to the 'ideological and legal' (i.e. insurgent and democratic) elements searching for a settlement to the Naga imbroglio. Moreover, the underground elements are divided into factions often along tribal denominations and are also engaged in factional feuds and conflicts for the dominance and control of Naga society and polity.[27] Scholars often argue that the fractures in the Naga society is a historical baggage having its source in the presence of countless tribes constituting the collective entity called Nagas[28] with some highlighting the point that the process of formation of new tribes is still continuing.[29]

This inter-tribal conflict and cohesion has substantial bearing on any analysis of the trends and outcome of electoral politics in the state of Nagaland and some authors argue, that politics in Nagaland is inter-tribal in character.[30] An example[31] can be cited from the parliamentary elections of 1977 when Mrs. Rano Shaiza contested the elections on a United Democratic Front ticket who despite being a niece of Mr. Phizo the father of the Naga Movement, was considered an "outsider" since she was considered a Tangkhul Naga from Manipur by virtue of her marriage to a Tangkhul Naga.

The inter-tribal rivalry and schism also gets reflected in electoral outcomes. During the 1984 elections to the Lok Sabha, for example, Chalie Kevichusa, an Angami from the Naga Nationalist Democratic Party (NNDP) lost the elections to the Congress-I (INC) candidate Chingwang Konyak by a margin of 1,37,182 votes. However, in the Angami dominated areas Kevichusa secured 3059 votes more than Chingwang.[32] This trend is visible also in the 1991 Lok Sabha elections when Imchalemba an Ao of the Nagaland People's Council (NPC) surpassed his INC rival Shikiho Sema by 19387 votes in areas dominated by the Ao tribe, while Shikiho a Sema polled 6519 votes more than Imchalemba in traditional Sema areas.[33] The trend continues during the 1996 Lok Sabha elections as well, when an independent candidate Khekiho from the Sema tribe polled 7247 votes more than his opponent Imchalemba an Ao, in Sema dominated areas.[34]

This inter-tribal schism and tribal factionalism is reflected not only in electoral outcomes and voting patterns but is an important component to Naga politics in general and influences all aspects of Naga society.[35] Some tribes, which consider them to have been 'fringed' in Naga politics, seem to have also realised the importance and effectiveness of electoral politics. This fact is reflected in the overwhelming participation of the Konyaks during the elections in 1998 when 72.71% (compared to the Lothas 3.80%) voting was reported from Konyak dominated areas[36] despite the general call for boycott of the elections by major traditional Naga bodies and institutions. Consequently electoral democracy in the state, like many of the other states in the region, consolidates inter-tribal differences and prioritises tribal identity as an important component of liberal democratic politics. In other words any serious assessment and understanding of the political history and evolution of the political community in the state must be able to view tribal identity as a central feature of politics in the state and indeed the region.

Electoral Politics in Nagaland: An Overview

Having emerged as a full-fledged state of the union of India on 1st December 1963, Nagaland got involved in electoral politics in January 1964 when the elections to the 40 members State Assembly were held for the first time. During these elections two state parties the Democratic Party under Kevichusa Angami and the Naga Nationalist Organisation under Shilu Ao contested the elections. The moderate faction of the NNC had formed the Democratic Party and its leaders Angami Kevishusa and Rano Shaiza were linked to the NNC. While the former had been a founder member of the NNC had argued at one time that "statehood was 'imposed' upon the Nagas"[37] while the latter happened to be Phizo's niece. During these elections the Democratic Party secured 12 seats while the rest went to the Naga Nationalist Organisation (NNO) of which 14 were secured uncontested. The Democratic Party, which contested the elections by "pledging peace and lasting good relationship with the government of India",[38] given the background of its leaders had the support of the underground elements[39] while the NNO was emphatically "committed to Nagaland's continuity with India".[40] In 1965, however, the members of the Democratic Party resigned *en bloc* and the party was dissolved when possibilities of Phizo's return became imminent.[41]

The 1969 elections to the 52 members[42] Legislative Assembly were contested by three political formations — the NNO which was a recognised regional party, the United Front of Nagaland (UFN) an unrecognised regional party and Independents. The UFN was basically a rechristened version of the Democratic Party and was composed of numerous erstwhile Democratic Party leaders including Kevichusa. During these elections many of the UFN candidates had open support from 'Oking'[43] and despite this fact had a "modest success" in the elections and could secure only 10 seats[44] in the legislative assembly. The NNO secured 22 seats and the Independents secured 8 seats.[45] The remaining 12 members were nominated from the Tuensang District.[46] This election was conducted in the backdrop of the Government of India's assertion that the "Naga problem was a local issue" and the "sovereignty of the government of India was indisputable"[47] and according to Chaube this stand of the government of India was strengthened by the victory of the NNO in the 1969 elections. The NNO with the support of 12 nominated members and 1 UFN defector formed the government headed by Hokishe Sema, who was known as "Indira man in Kohima". However, the issue of 'political solution' of the Naga problem, which by now had acquired the potential of becoming an important political tool and resource for detractors to legitimise their personal political grudges, became an issue that led to the dropping of two influential leaders — T.N. Angami and S.C. Jamir — which subsequently led to the formation of the United Democratic Front (UDF) comprising of the members of the erstwhile United Front and the NNO defectors.[48]

Thus politics of defections had arrived in Nagaland and this influenced the outcome of the elections to the Legislative Assembly in 1974. The UDF by obtaining 30.01% of the total votes polled secured 25 seats while the NNO obtaining 35.71% of the total votes polled secured 23 seats and the Independents secured 12 seats with 34.28% of the vote share.[49] Though the UDF under the leadership of Vizol formed the government with the help of 7 independents, 6 of whom became ministers, the government lost its majority in March 1975 to the NNO, which increased its strength again by engineering defections on the "question of the release of political prisoners".[50] Though J.C. Jasokie formed the NNO dominated government, the stability of the government had been fragile and state was placed under President's rule in March 1975 and the Assembly kept in suspended animation to be dissolved on May 20, 1975.

The elections to the Legislative Assembly of 1977 was conducted in the backdrop of the Shillong Accord[51] that sought to consolidate the "democratic experiment" pursued by the government of India to resolve the Naga crisis. This accord however, not only served as an effort to consolidate the democratic institutions and culture but also resulted in a split in the underground movement and the emergence of the National Socialist Council of Nagaland[52] (NSCN), which emphasised its intention to establish a "Nagaland for Christ". Scholars like Misra argue that this was another instance of the gradual narrowing down of the popular base of the underground movement.[53] For purposes of this study it may not be wrong to argue that this emphasis of the NSCN helped to not only fracture Naga society along Christian/non-Christian lines but also establish religion as an influential factor in electoral politics of the state.

It was also during these elections that for the first time a national party — the Indian National Congress — contested the elections, which saw the merger of the pro-Congress NNO with the Congress and together they contested 37 seats winning 15 seats from 20.44% of the votes polled mostly from the *Sema* and mixed tribes inhabited areas. The UDF winning 39 seats of the 60 contested polled 39.23% of the votes formed the government headed by veteran Naga leader Vizol. The UDF secured most of its seats in *Thankul, Ao* and *Chakesang* dominated areas. However, on April 1980, S.C. Jamir quit the government to form the United Legislature Party and later to join the Indian National Congress. In that same year Jasolie who was elected on a Congress ticket quit the party to establish, along with the UDF, the Naga National Democratic Party (NNDP).

In the elections to the Legislative Assembly in 1982, the Congress and the NNDP secured 24 seats each with 32.08% and 32.01%[54] of the votes polled respectively. The Congress managed to obtain the support of the 12 Independent candidates and formed the government headed by S.C. Jamir who was replaced by Hokishe Sema in Oct 1986 amidst widespread allegations and charges of corruption and political opportunism. During the period between 1986 and 1993, Nagaland was witness to a constant state of instability, which culminated in the frequent imposition of President's rule in the state.

Amidst the instability and charges of corruption and escalation of violence, the elections to the sixth Legislative Assembly were held in 1987. Writers[55] maintain that during these elections an estimated 6–10 crores were spent by political parties to sway political opinion and votes of the electorate. The Congress secured 34 seats with 39.84% of the votes polled, the NNDP secured 18 seats with 30.33% of the votes polled, the Nagaland Peoples Party along with numerous Congress dissidents contested 32 seats to secure only 1 seat with 9.03% of the votes polled and the Independents won 7 seats with 20.61% of the votes polled.[56] The Bharatiya Janata Party contested the state elections for the first time in 2 seats but could not secure any of them. Like all the previous elections in the state, during these elections also the underground played an influential role and underground activists manned large sections of the NNDP leadership, even the Congress list was supposed to have contained several NSCN activists.[57] Prominent leaders of the Congress like "Hokishe Sema attended largely publicised prayer meeting with the members of the NSCN", thus leading to assertions by writers like Misra that by playing to the underground interests the Congress neutralised the NNDP's claim to represent the underground interests. This aspect is an important indicator to the fact that by now the relations between the 'underground' and the 'overground' was no longer an anathema in democratic politics as had been the case in the late sixties when allegations of such linkages between legal representatives and the underground lead many elected members to openly renounce their membership of Phizo's NNC.[58]

Amidst political uncertainty and instability, elections to the Legislative Assembly was held again in 1989 where the Congress secured 36 seats with 51.45% of the vote share and state party like the Naga Peoples Council (NPC) won 24 with 41.61% of the votes polled. In the 1993 elections to the legislative assembly, the BJP again contested the elections but secured no seat with 0.35% of the votes polled. The Congress secured 35 seats with 46.02% of the votes polled, the NPC secured 17 seats with 32.82% of the vote share, the Democratic Labour Party (DLP) an unrecognised party secured 1 seat with 0.51% of the vote share and Independents with 20.29% of the vote share secured 7 seats.

The Legislative Assembly elections of 1998 were held amidst a boycott call by the Naga Hoho and other Naga organisations.[59] The two major regional political formations — the Nagaland People's Council and the Nagaland Democratic Movement as well as a national party like the BJP supported the boycott call and no members from these parties filed any nominations.[60] The Nagaland Baptist Church Council (NBCC) the largest religious-civic body in the state supported the call for poll boycott and issued an "Agenda for Peace" that was endorsed by the NSCN. The boycott call was made in support of the demand for political dialogue between the Government of India and the Insurgents to end the five-decade old Naga imbroglio,[61] unencumbered by elections. Surprisingly, the sitting Congress Lok Sabha member also declined to participate in the elections and sought deferment of the polls.[62] In spite of the boycott call, the Congress party emphasised the need to participate in the elections, which they felt would in no way obstruct the political dialogue.[63] Nonetheless, feeling the pulse of the electorate the Congress declared, among other issues, its commitment to a policy of "reconciliation among various groups and support for Naga unity"; "and permanent resolution of the Naga problem within A.D. 2000 through peaceful means of dialogue and negotiation among the contesting parties."[64]

Thus in a situation where other political parties refrained from contesting the elections the Congress Party secured 53 seats that include 43 candidates who were returned uncontested to the assembly due to the absence of any other political party. Among the 20 Independents who contested the elections seven were declared elected.[65] In fact, elections, in the true sense of the term, took place only in 17 constituencies. The Lok Sabha Seat was also won by the Congress candidate K. Asangba Sangtam.

Assembly Elections-2003: Issues, Trends and Politics

The elections to the 10th Legislative Assembly of Nagaland held in February 2003 must be analysed in the background of the ongoing peace negotiations between the government of India and one of the dominant underground groups the NSCN-IM. This has bearing not only as a political issue determining the future path of Naga politics and society but also due to the fact that these 'underground elements' play significant roles in determining electoral outcomes. Though the 'collective leadership' of the NSCN-IM maintained their unwillingness to 'participate' in the elections they however, categorically emphasised that they will not disrupt the polling process in the state.[66] This practically indicates a softening of their "commitment to a sovereign, independent Nagalim" and an urge to solve the Naga imbroglio through political negotiations. However groups like the NNC 'unreservedly' condemned[67] the elections as an institutional ploy by the Indian state to integrate the Nagas, while the other major player, the NSCN-K choose to maintain an ominous silence on its stand on the elections.

225 candidates, for the 60-member assembly, contested these elections that saw a new alignment of 'political' forces in the state.[68] While the recognised national parties like the Indian National Congress-I (INC), the Bharatiya Janata Party (BJP), and the National Congress Party (NCP) had put up a total of 105 candidates, regional parties together put up 81 members followed by other state parties, 22 and Independents 17. As results in the Table 1 shows, of the 60 seats, the INC won 21 seats securing approximately 35 % of the vote share on the seats contested, the NPF won 19 seats with 31.66% vote share, the BJP 7 seats with 11.66% of the vote share, NDM won 5 seats with 8.33% of the vote share, INDs 4 seats with 6.66% of the vote share, JD (U) 3 seats with 5% of the vote share and the Samata Party (SAP) won 1 seat

Table 1: Detailed results of the Legislative Assembly elections in Nagaland from 1964–2003

Year	Party	Seats Won	Votes share
1964	NNO	28	NA
	DP	12	NA
	Total	40	
1969	NNO	22	38.66%
	UFN	10	21.76%
	IND	8	39.58%
	Total	40*	
1974	NNO	23	35.71%
	UDF	25	30.01%
	IND	12	34.28%
	Total	60	
1977	INC	15	20.44%
	UDF	39	39.23%
	NCN	1	11.85%
	IND	5	28.48%
	Total	60	
1982	INC	24	32.08%
	NND	24	32.01%
	IND	12	35.91%
	Total	60	
1987	INC	34	39.84%
	BJP	NIL	0.19%
	NNDP	18	30.33%
	NPP	1	9.03%
	IND	7	20.61%
	Total	26	
1989	INC	36	51.45%
	NPC	24	41.61%
	NPP	NIL	2.75%
	IND	NIL	4.19%
	Total	60	
1993	INC	35	46.02%
	BJP	NIL	0.35%
	NPC	17	32.82%
	DLP	1	0.51%
	IND	7	20.29%
	Total	25	

(contd.)

(contd. Table 1)

Year	Party	Seats Won	Votes share
1998	INC	53	50.73%
	IND	7	49.27%
	Total	60	
2003	INC	21	35.85%
	BJP	7	10.87%
	JD(U)	3	5.80%
	SAP	1	1.18%
	NPF	19	29.77%
	NDM	5	9.52%
	IND	4	4.42%
	NCP	NIL	2.00%
	AITC	NIL	0.33%
	RLD	NIL	0.20%
	NLDP	NIL	0.05%
	Total	60	

* The total seats to the Legislative Assembly were 52 of which 12 members were to be nominated from the Tuensang District. In other words only 40 of the seats were contestable.

with 1% of the vote share. Parties like the NCP secured only 2% of the votes share and could not secure any seat. It is interesting to note that in a state where a substantial majority of the people are perceived as "anti-Indian", 48.72% of the electors voted in favour of the National Parties, 39.34% of the electors supporting the registered regional political formations, 7.51% supporting candidates of parties from other states and 4.42% expressing their support for the independents. Opposition parties that had boycotted elections to the 9th Legislative Assembly in 1998 on the slogan, "Solution not Election", had during these elections realised the political implications of participation in the institutional mechanism and seemed to have transformed that slogan into "Elections for Solution". Consequently, the defeat of the S.C. Jamir led INC government had been the main agenda of the combined strength of the opposition led by the newly formed Nagaland People Front (NPF). Though the substantial strength of this new party was mainly due to the joining of numerous colleagues, of Mr. S.C. Jamir, like Mr. Neiphiu Rio the home minister, the party had veterans of Naga politics like Mr. Vizol. It is important to recall here that it was this individual along with Mr. Jamir who had ventured to engage the might of the Indian state on its own turf by contesting elections and capturing power[69] through the United Front of Nagaland later re-christened the United Democratic Front (UDF), in 1974 and 1977.

The formation of the Democratic Alliance of Nagaland (DAN) in Jan. 2003 initially through the combined efforts of the NPF, BJP, JD(U), and Samata Party, virtually sealed the fate of "Mr Jamir's INC" in these 10th elections to the assembly. However, the real contest had taken place between the INC and the NPF (Table 2 for a comparison).

Though many observers, this author has spoken to, feel that party politics as an ideological phenomenon, plays an insignificant role in the outcome of the elections in the state where tribe affiliations, tribal chiefs and the armed groups play a more dominant role, political parties did issue manifestoes and common minimum programmes.

While the manifestoes of all parties spoke about a solution to the vexed Naga problem the INC manifesto highlighted the personal role of S.C. Jamir in being the main facilitator in the process of peace by withdrawing the warrants of arrest against the NSCN-IM leaders despite attempts on his life by the members of the group. It also highlighted the fact that any solution to the Naga problem is being undermined by the presence of substantial differences between the various Naga tribes and their respective representative affiliations and thus urged for unity among the various groups prior to any settlement. In this context it may be worthwhile to recall that divisions in the "Naga society" though represented by the presence of two major 'insurgent elements' — the NSCN-IM and the NSCN-K along with the NNC — is merely an organised reflection of the deep internal tribal rivalries and divisions. This seems to have acquired institutional form also in the state structures where the *Ao* tribe is perceived to have control over the bureaucracy, while the *Angamis, Semas, Chakhesang* and *Lothas* are perceived to be the other major players in the polity. These divisions are so important that any government policy prescriptions and political decisions are implemented by paying due consideration to the interests of the different Naga tribes and effectively recognising the different tribes as formal political units.[70] Though all the political parties understand and respect this reality, the INC sought to confront this issue directly. Therefore, in July 2000, the NPCC-I issued a booklet entitled,

Table 2: Vote Share of Parties in Constituencies-2003

Constituencies	BJP	INC	NPF	NDM	JD(U)	IND	NCP	AITC	SAP	RLD	NLDP
Dimapur-I	52.69%	28.68%	11.28%	—	2.43%	4.85%	—	—	—	—	—
Dimapur-II	6.33%	45.57%	48.18%	—	—	—	—	—	—	—	—
Dimapur-III	—	6.90%	44.04%	46.05%	—	3.00%					
Ghaspani-I	10.15%	21.38%	50.98%	—	17.47%						
Ghaspani-II	—	30.20%	18.88%	28.45%	20.13%	2.13%					
Tening	15.25%	35.16%	23.03%	7.50%	19.03%						
Peren	—	35.62%	42.10%	6.19%			16.06				
Western Angami	6.57%	32.75%	40.23%			20.45%					
Kohima Town		42.21%	44.87%	12.91%							
Northern Angami-I		46.08%	53.91%								
Northern Angami-II	3.86%	26.09%	67.59%			2.44%					
Tseminyu	5.19%	30.89%	21.62%		38.90%		3.37%				
Southern Angami-I		30.23%	25.66%			19.95%		24.14%			
Pughoboto	6.64%	39.39%	4.67%		49.27%						
Pfutsero		41.76%	51.04%	7.19%							
Chizami		28.34%	23.23%				13.70%		34.71%		
Chazouba	6.99%	24.96%	35.84%			24.51%	7.66%				
Phek		40.88%	59.11%								
Meluri	10.37%	35.97%	41.37%							12.27%	
Tuli		57.71%	42.28%								
Arkakong	0.18%	51.51%	48.22%								
Impur		58.05%	41.94%								
Angetyongpang	3.87%	19.46%	3.96%		17.27%	42.16%			13.24%		
Mongoya	2.33%	67.62%	30.03%								
Aonglenden		90.07%	9.59%			0.33%					
Mokokchung Town		53.62%	46.37%								

Koridang	14.03%	40.31%	3.19%			42.44%					
Jangpetkong		74.08%	17.52%						8.39%		
Alongtaki	59.80%	40.19%									
Akuluto		45.57%	44.42%								
Atoizu		33.68%	33.49%	32.82%							
Suruhoto	15.79%	27.06%		11.55%		45.27%					0.31%
Aghunato		54.55%	0.32%	45.11%							
Zunheboto	11.48%	43.65%		44.86%							
Sataka	1.73%	40.88%	32.86%	24.51%							
Tyui	33.56%	49.51%	16.92%								
Wokha Town	35.33%	16.08%	24.35%				24.22%				
Sanis	4.15%	8.73%	26.75%	17.00%	11.26%		26.56%	3.51%			1.98%
Bhandari	5.63%	27.03%	14.12%	31.10%					21.95%	0.13%	
Tizit	2.05%	28.00%	39.31%	29.60%	1.20%						
Wakching	52.00%	47.99%									
Tapi	9.98%	30.58%	32.30%	27.12%							
Phomching		59.22%	30.52%	5.64%	4.55%						
Tehok	2.47%	52.61%	36.87%	7.06%						0.96%	
Mon Town	3.25%	44.27%	33.08%	6.98%		12.39%					
Aboi	34.64	21.69%	43.62%				0.03%				
Moka		33.78%	46.05%	20.15%							
Tobu	4.94%	43.28%	48.22%			3.54%					
Tamlu	1.88%	31.32%	15.57%	29.73%	21.47%						
Longleng	24.06%	23.14%	25.27%		27.51%						
Noksen		56.16%	43.83%								
Longkhim Chare	50.85%	49.14%									
Tuensang Sadar-I	6.65%	36.86%	11.77%	7.49%		37.20%					
Tuensang Sadar-II	35.94%	31.94%		32.10%							
Noklak		45.49%	54.44%			0.05%					

(contd.)

(contd. Table 2)

Constituencies	BJP	INC	NPF	NDM	JD(U)	IND	NCP	AITC	SAP	RLD	NLDP
Thononkyu	9.21%	18.49%	8.33%	36.06%	13.72%	14.16%					
Shamator Chessore	8.59%	30.49%	29.01%	10.58%		21.32%					
Seyochung Sitimi	0.93%	30.33%	4.40%	64.32%							
Pungro Kiphire	47.12%	11.14%	41.72%								

"Bedrock of Naga Society",[71] that sought to question the reality of the claim that "Nagas were an independent *nation* since time immemorial" and emphasised the fact that it was the 16-Point Agreement, which laid the foundation of a 'collective Naga' society and identity. However, this proved to be a political miscalculation for the INC because the booklet invited widespread criticism from the major players in Naga society like the Naga Hoho, student bodies, insurgent groups, and sections of the intelligentsia.

This had also been a major issue in the elections and the NPF vehemently contested this claim and cited it as another stumbling block initiated by Jamir to stall the peace negotiations. The NPF urged the 'Naga citizens' to realise that mere statehood was not the final solution to the Naga problem[72] and thus its manifesto requested a mandate from the people to go deeper in achieving the desired goals of the people. The rhetorical ambiguity of this stand on statehood also probably reflects our earlier argument regarding the 'legitimation dilemma' among the legal and extra-legal forces in the state seeking legitimacy and loyalty of the Naga people. The NPF by questioning the actual status and role of statehood subtly injected the issue of self-determination into the political agenda. Moreover, the NPF while calling for unity among the numerous Naga tribes highlighted the role of the INC and Mr. Jamir in actually creating divisions among tribes giving the case of the *Chakhesangs'* as an instance.[73]

These tribal divisions and their importance in politics can also be discerned by assessing the electoral role of the respective tribes in their areas of habitation. If we look at the candidates from the various constituencies we find that members of the dominant tribes of the area are the contestants and the winners. This demonstrates that it is mainly tribe affiliation and not party affiliation that determines the outcome of the elections. Moreover, an assessment of the social profile of the candidates reflects that the *Semas* have a respectable edge over other tribes in the overall results tally followed by the *Aos, Angamis, Chakhesang* and others in descending order. Moreover, instances of open proclamation of support by some tribes for particular candidates[74] reflect the collective pressure exerted by the community for a supposedly individual choice and decision.

Besides the emphasis on a "comprehensive political solution" to the Naga problem and "calls for unity"[75] among the Naga tribes the political discourse dwelt on other areas like health, economy, employment, formation of women department etc. but they received only a routine mention without any clear blueprint for action and played almost an insignificant role in public rallies of the various parties.[76] However, the Nationalist Democratic Movement (NDM) that won 5 seats in these elections made a special mention of the "Indigenous Minorities" like the *Kukis, Garos, Kacharis* and *Nepalis* and promised measures for safeguarding their rights. This is significant not only for the state but for the entire region as a whole because 'indigenity' in the region had acquired almost a hegemonic instrument for dominant groups in the region. In this background the assertion for the protection of 'indigenous minority' groups of the state is a bold political initiative, which even the national parties are wary of proclaiming. Another issue that strikes an emotional chord among the Nagas is the "call for integration of all Naga people", so while regional party like the NPF innocuously emphasised its commitment "to the integration of Nagas", the NDM emphasised "integration of all contiguous Naga areas" as its political goal. However, national parties like the INC and the BJP avoided any mention of an issue that has immense implications for the territorial jurisdiction of other northeastern states.

A significant aspect of electoral politics in Nagaland is that despite the effective intervention of the Naga Mothers' Union and Women in general towards Naga unity and efforts for peace and even commitment for the establishment of women department by political parties, none of the parties considered it worthwhile to nominate a substantial number of women candidates. Therefore, the NPF fielded a lone woman while the other two women in the electoral race contested the elections as Independents, though none of them were elected to the assembly.[77] Significantly, Nagaland has had no women members to the Legislative Assembly since 1964 and since then only 10 women have actually contested polls in the state.[78] This is also surprising because of the fact that at least in seven assembly segments women voters outnumber the male voters and constitute 48% of the state's total electorate.[79]

It has often been argued that "general elections in Nagaland deals with Christian political leaders and electorate"[80] and the active participation of church leaders in election campaigns and rallies of political parties along with issuing directives by denominational church forums[81] amply demonstrate this reality. Though other political parties refrained from any overt emphasis, on this aspect the BJP did not fail to derive mileage from this religious polarity in the state and honestly highlighted the issue of P.C. Alexander, a Christian, promoted as a presidential candidate[82] by the BJP, who was opposed by the Congress-I. In this context it may be mentioned that many observers were surprised at the winning of 6 seats by the BJP in a "Christian state",[83] but it is important to recall our earlier arguments that lack of ideological politics and importance of tribe affiliations play a significant role in the outcome of election rather than party affiliations. But not to deny the BJP its due, it must be mentioned that like all the other opposition parties, the BJP also derived aid from highlighting the role of the Prime Minister Atal Bihari Vajpayee in showing political maturity by inviting the NSCN –IM leaders to India for peace negotiations. Besides role and personality of the veteran Naga leader, Hokishe Sema who joined the BJP in 1999 helping to secure for the BJP an overwhelming mandate cannot be underestimated. It may be mentioned here that the national parties that include the BJP, the INC and the NCP together polled 48.72% of the total valid votes in the state compared to the regional combine that polled only 39.34% of the total valid votes (Table 3).

Table 3: Percentage of Votes Polled by Parties

National Parties	Parties from other States	Regional Parties of the State	Independents
BJP/INC/ NCP	SAP/JD(U)/ RLD/AITC	NPF/NDM/ NLDP	IND
48.72%	7.51%	39.34%	4.42%

As highlighted earlier, the role of armed groups in these elections as well was a major issue. Here as well traditional tribal rivalries reflected their influence and we find that while the Congress-I claimed the interference of the NSCN-IM, its traditional rival led by a *Thankul* and *Sema* Naga from Manipur, the opposition claimed the role of the NSCN-K, led by a *Nemi* Naga and supported by the *Aos* and the *Angamis* in influencing the prospects of Mr. Jamir and the INC.[84] While the NSCN-IM is seen as responsible for the abduction and intimidation of Congress-I voters and workers[85] the NSCN-K issued threats to newly elected members of the opposition from entering their areas of operation.[86] Despite denials by the involved political parties, it may be interesting to analyse the coincidence that the main opposition party NPF bagged the maximum number of seats in the southern parts of the state which are considered the traditional support base of the NSCN-IM, while the INC bagged most of its seats in areas dominated by the NSCN-K. Consequently, while the NPF and the opposition received majority support from the *Semas, Chakhesang*, and *Zeliangs* dominating the southern part of the state, the INC received support from the *Aos, Konyaks, Angamis*, and *Lothas* and this is reflected by the tribe affiliation of members elected from the respective parties to the 10th assembly.

Nonetheless, the elections to the 10th Legislative Assembly saw an increased fervour among the electorate for participation in the electoral processes of the state. This is a notable indication for democratic politics and a significant pointer to the benefits of political engagement for a 'comprehensive solution' to the Naga political problem.

In trying to assess the effects of electoral democracy in Nagaland certain general conclusions can be drawn from the trends and patterns of participation of the electorate and the influence and role of numerous state and non-state actors in the election processes. It may be argued that, " elections are used as instruments by various sections of the society to convert their political resources and power into authority"[87] and in a social condition where tribe affiliations, inter-tribe coalitions and rivalry are considered important social assets, elections provide a mechanism where these assets can be transformed into effective political power that controls and directs state authority. Moreover in the state of Nagaland, the legal distinction between actors affiliated to the 'underground' or the 'overground' is often blurred and we find, as detailed in the preceding pages, that the actors affiliated to the 'underground' have often sought to legitimise their relevance by contesting the elections. Whether this is a positive indicator of the success of democratic politics will depend on our description and definition of the concept of self-determination and constitutional obligation. Moreover, the concern for a "political solution" to the Naga imbroglio has also become a political tool exploited by parties of regional or national orientation in electoral contests in the state,

Table 4: Index of Political Parties

Bharatiya Janata Party	BJP
Indian National Congress	INC
Nationalist Congress Party	NCP
Samata Party	SAP
Rashtriya Lok Dal	RLD
Janata Dal (United)	JD(U)
All India Trinamool Congress	AITC
Nagaland People's Front	NPF
Nationalist Democratic Movement	NDM
Nagaland Democratic Party	NLDP

though it is difficult to interpret what a "political solution" would imply for the Naga polity as well as the Indian union.

Nonetheless, in spite of the emergence of negative consequences[88] of the decades old conflict in the state there seems to be a widening of the democratic space that is aided immensely by the various civil society institutions like the Naga Hoho, Naga Mothers' Union, the Church Forum, Student Federation and the intelligentsia. The mediating and interventionist role of these organisations in their efforts to seek 'self-determination through democratic politics' for the Naga people is in fact an obvious reflection of the subtle but significant shift in the political intention and objective of the Naga electorate.

NOTES AND REFERENCES

1. This boycott of the elections was against the forcible incorporation of Naga dominated areas into India. See Udayan Misra. *The Periphery Strikes Back: Challenges to the Nation-State in Assam & Nagaland* (IIAS: Shimla, 2000).
2. S.K. Chaube, *Hill Politics in Northeast India* (Orient Longman Ltd. Hyderabad.) 1999, reprint. p. 16.
3. The three members were Khelhoshe Sema, Chubatensu Ao and Satsuo Angami. See *Report on the* 1st *General Elections, 1963* (Chief Electoral Officer, Kohima 1964), p. 2.
4. For instance the Peace Mission comprising B.P. Chaliha, Jayaprakash Narayan and Rev Michael Scott in 1964 and the numerous ceasefire agreements between the GOI and the Naga insurgents along with efforts by numerous civil society organisations.
5. The total area of the state is 16,579 sq kms, comprised of 8 districts and a total population of 19,88,636 (census-2001). The total electorate of the state in 2003 was 10,13,799 (see Facts at a Glance). General Elections to 10th Nagaland Legislative Assembly 2003 (Election Dept. Government of Nagaland, Jun. 2003).

6. Dr. M. Aram quoted in Chaube *loc. cit.*, p. 166.
7. Misra. *op. cit.*, p. 46.
8. The term has been used from Rekha Chowdhary and Nagendra Rao. "Elections 2002: Implications for Politics of Separatism". *Economic & Political Weekly*, January 4–10, 2003.
9. See *Statistical Report on General Elections 1964 to the Nagaland Legislative Assembly*. http://www.eci.gov.in.op.
10. Udayon Misra, *The Periphery Strikes op. cit.*, p. 56.
11. See for example Nagaland Elections. *Economic & Political Weekly*. No. 5, Dec. 19, 1987, p. 2194.
12. See Udayon Misra, *North East India: Quest for Identity* (Omsons Publications, Delhi, 1988), p. 2.
13. Misra *op. cit.*, 2000, p. 27.
14. See. Rajesh Dev *Politics of Difference: A Study of Ethno-Nationalism with Reference to the Chicanos and the Nagas* (Unpublished Ph.D Thesis. NEHU 2002), p. 83.
15. *Ibid.*
16. For a discussion on the Moderate and Extremist Factions of Naga Politics, See Chaube, *op. cit.* 1999 pp. 158–162, or Misra *op. cit.* 2000, pp. 31–34.
17. See L.N. Luthra. *Nagaland from a District to a State* (DIPR. Arunachal Pradesh, Shillong 1974), p. 22.
18. See Chaube *op. cit.* 1999, p. 162. The three members were Khelhoshe Sema, Chubatensu Ao and Satsuo Angami. See *Report on the 1st General Elections, 1963* (Chief Electoral Officer, Kohima 1964), p. 2.
19. See B. Datta Ray and S.P. Agarwal. *Reorganisation of Northeast India since 1947* (Concept Publishing House, N. Delhi, 1994), p. 246.
20. Udayan Misra. "Naga Peace Talks: High Hopes and Hard Realities." *Economic & Political Weekly*. February 15–21, 2003, pp. 593–597.
21. See "NPF leaders upbeat on Polls". *Eastern Mirror*, February 5, 2003.
22. Misra. *op. cit.* 2000. p. 56
23. See Sanjay Hazarika. *Strangers of the Mist* (Penguin Books India Ltd: N. Delhi, 1994), p. 240.
24. Chaube. *op. cit.*, 1999. p. 169.
25. Misra. *op. cit.*, 1987. p. 2193.
26. See "NSCN rebels held from minister's car" *Hindustan Times, North East Special*, May 7, 2003. p. 1.
27. For example the conflicts between the NSCN-IM and NSCN-K the NFG and the NNC (Adino) all representing different factions and tribes of the Naga society.
28. See Dev, *op. cit.* 2002, p. 26.
29. See Pusa, *op. cit.* 1996, p. 6.
30. *Ibid.*, pp. 143–145.
31. S.K. Chaube, *Electoral Politics in Northeast India* (Universities Press. Madras, 1985), pp. 166–167.
32. See *Lok Sabha General Elections 1984. Detail Election Results* (Chief Electoral Officer, Kohima, Nagaland, 1985) pp. 152–156.
33. See *Report on the Tenth General Election to the House of the People from the Nagaland Parliamentary Constituency. 1991* (Dept. of Secretary, Election. Government of Nagaland, Kohima, 1991), pp. 252–256.

34. See *Report on the Eleventh General Elections to the Lok Sabha, 1996 from the Nagaland Parliamentary Constituency* (Chief Electoral Officer, Kohima), p. 75.
35. See for example Chaube *op. cit.* 1985. pp. 163–171.
36. *Nagaland Post.* No. 62 (Dimapur, February 26, 1998), p. 1.
37. See. Nirmal Nibedon. *Nagaland — The Night of the Guerrillas* (Lancer. N. Delhi, 2000 reprint), p. 108.
38. Chaube. *op. cit.* 1999, p. 165.
39. Misra. *op. cit.* 1987, p. 2193.
40. Chaube. *op. cit.* 1999, p. 165.
41. Nibedon. *op. cit.*, p. 108.
42. The number of seats in the assembly was initially 40 in 1964, increased to 52 in 1969 and to 60 in 1974. See *Handbook — General Elections 1998* (Published by the Chief Electoral Officer, Nagaland).
43. Nibedon. *op. cit.*, 2000. p. 231.
44. See *Election Commission of India — State Election, 1969 to the Legislative Assembly of Nagaland.* http://www.eci.gov.in
45. *Ibid.*, p. 4.
46. See Nibedon. *op. cit.*, 2000. p. 231.
47. Chaube. *op. cit.*, 1999. p. 169.
48. *Ibid.*, p. 170.
49. See *Election Commission of India — State Election, 1974 to the Legislative Assembly of Nagaland.* http://www.eci.gov.in.
50. See Chaube *op. cit.*, 1985. p. 165.
51. See Misra. *op. cit.*, 2000. p. 207.
52. Now referred to as National Socialist Council of Nagalim.
53. Misra. *op. cit.* 2000, p. 51.
54. See *Election Commission of India — State Election, 1982 to the Legislative Assembly of Nagaland.* http://www.eci.gov.in
55. Misra 1987, *op. cit.*, p. 2337.
56. See *Election Commission of India — State Election, 1987 to the Legislative Assembly of Nagaland.* http://www.eci.gov.in
57. Misra. *op. cit.* 1987, p. 2338.
58. See Nibedon *op. cit.*, 2000, p. 231.
59. See *Nagaland Post.* December 19, 1997, p. 1.
60. See *Nagaland Post.* February 2, 1998, p. 1.
61. See *Nagaland Post.* December 19, 1997, p. 1
62. See *Nagaland Post.* January 24, 1998. p. 8.
63. See *Nagaland Post.* January 23, 1998, p. 1.
64. See *Manifesto of the 1998 Elections* (NPCC. Kohima), p. 8.
65. See *Election Commission of India — State Election, 1998 to the Legislative Assembly of Nagaland.* http://www.eci.gov.in
66. See "Northeast India rebels say Delhi talks doomed" www.khaleejtimes.co.ae/ktarchive/130103/subcont.htm
67. See "NNC condemns state elections, warns Nagas". *Northeast Herald.* February 24, 2003.
68. The number of seats in the assembly was initially 40 in 1964, increased to 52 in 1969 and to 60 in 1974. See *Handbook — General Elections 1998* (Published by the Chief Electoral Officer, Nagaland).
69. Hazarika. *op. cit.* 1994, p. 107.
70. See Pusa. *op. cit.* 1996, p. 123.

71. See "Bedrock of Naga Society" (Published by NPCC-I. Kohima, 2000).
72. See "NPF leaders upbeat on Polls". *Eastern Mirror,* February 5, 2003.
73. See " Therie charges booklet, Congress". *Eastern Mirror,* February 6, 2003.
74. See "Chakhesang community declares support" *Eastern Mirror.* February 15, 2003.
75. Resolutions to bring Nagas Areas together were passed thrice by the state assembly in December 1964; August 1970 and September 1994. Recently in December 2003, the Assembly again passed a resolution calling for the integration of Naga dominated areas.
76. If we glean through the pages of the Eastern Mirror, Nagaland Page, and Northeast Herald all published from the state, we find that there is very little emphasis on these issues except of course only as a means to highlight the corrupt rule of the Congress-I.
77. The three women candidates were Anupama Mech an Independent from Dimapur-III (ST) receiving only 427 votes; Akheli also an Independent from Ghaspani-II (ST) receiving 486 votes and Chubalemla of the NPF from Aonglenden (ST) receiving only 928 votes.
78. See. "Nagaland continues to have no-woman house", *Eastern Mirror,* March 4, 2003.
79. *Ibid.*
80. See. L. Bizo Chairman of the Joint Church Forum. *Eastern Mirror,* February 8, 2003.
81. See. "Chakhesangs Support". *Eastern Mirror,* February 13, 2003.
82. See " BJP MPs visit Wokha district". *Eastern Mirror,* February 5, 2003.
83. According to the Census of India 1991, the Christian population constitute 87.46% of the total population.
84. See. "NSCN-IM Interference in Polls — Jamir". *Northeast Herald,* February 8, 2003.
85. See, besides other news reports. "NSCN-IM cadres on the run". *Northeast Herald,* February 24, 2003.
86. See "Legislators warned to 'keep off'". *Eastern Mirror,* March 4, 2003.
87. See Subrata Mitra, *Culture & Rationality* (Sage India, N. Delhi), p. 131.
88. See Hazarika. *op. cit.* 1994, pp. 240–242.

Ethnic Groups, Electoral Politics and Democratic Consensus in Tripura

*Rajesh Dev** and *Manas Paul**

"Tripura — the original land of the tribal people — is also the house of the non-tribals and people of different religious faiths",[1] is how one author describes the character of the state. This statement also, however, gives us a subtle indication of the unease associated with the fact that, though the state is the original homeland of the tribal people, is now equally claimed by the non-tribes as well. Consequently the emerging conflict of values and claims by democratic and armed actors representing the interests of the respective groups are embroiled in fractious confrontation. This confrontation is exhibited not only in the conflict and violence unleashed by the armed groups but also in the democratic space where the political discourse circulates around ethnic interests. Therefore, in an analysis of the condition of representational politics in the state it is important to acknowledge the impact and importance of the ethnic polarisation. In fact we may not be too far from truth to assert that competitive politics has not merely aggravated armed violence in the state but has become an important appendage to the structures of administration where ethnic divisions are becoming institutionalised. This fact is reflected in the overwhelming control of the tribal armed groups during the elections to the tribal autonomous councils where insurgent-backed groups take over power through 'democratic means'.[2]

---

* An earlier version of this paper was published in the *Economic and Political Weekly*, Vol. 15, April 12, 2003.

The ethnic polarisation in the state of Tripura is considered to have its origin in the 'divide and rule' policy adopted by the 'tribal' king who was responsible for not only encouraging settlement of the non-tribal population in his plain territories,[3] but simultaneously encouraging ethnic and communal politics through deliberate policy prescriptions.[4] Therefore, political movements in Tripura slowly assumed three distinct ideological paths. It has been pointed out that "the *Tripura Rajya Ganaparishad* and later the State Congress Committee tried to follow the all-India nationalist approach, the *Janamangal-Janasiksha Samiti-Prajamandal* and later its offshoot the Communist Party adopted progressive leftist approach, the *Tripur Sangha, Anjuman Islamia, Hindu Mahasabha* etc."[5] concentrated their claims along communal and ethnic alignments. Slowly as the process for the emergence of the new state began, these divisions impelled by sociological and economic determinants took the form of armed confrontation that further got polarised along ethnic lines.

In its transformation from being a Part C state where democracy took the form of people being associated with the administration in an "advisory rather than directive capacity",[6] to "the struggle for responsible government"[7] through a full-fledged state ultimately established on January 21, 1972, the hill people of Tripura kept themselves away[8] from any political movements. However, the establishment of a full-fledged state ensured democratic participation of all the people of Tripura in a "directive capacity" through electoral politics. Consequently the elections to the Legislative Assembly for 60 seats took place in 1972. The distribution of seats and constituencies were made keeping in view the ethnic and demographic profile of the state and thus 36 seats were placed under the general category, 19 were reserved for the Scheduled Tribes category and 5 seats for the Scheduled Castes. Though the people began to be engaged in electoral politics since the 1952 elections to the Lok Sabha the reorganisation of state in 1972 as a full-fledged state of the Indian union brought the people in direct contact with representative politics.

An analysis of the elections results and trends in the state since 1952 clearly reveals the fact that though there was a presence of numerous political formations, the electoral victories were shared mostly between the Congress and the Communist Party.[9] After the partition, the Bengali Hindu refugees from Bangladesh outnumbered the Tripuris or "*Twipras*" who had been the dominant people until 1947. This according to scholars caused serious changes in the socio-economic and political life-patterns of the indigenous peoples.[10] Consequently, Chaube argues that as the incoming refugees started to settle and began to influence electoral results, the Congress was preferred as the party that could form the state government, while the Communists were preferred as representatives to the Lok Sabha.[11] The Congress, however, in spite of numerous odds it had been facing at the national level along with the rise of regional parties in the states had been successful in wresting both the seats to the Lok Sabha from the Communists in 1967.[12] The Congress also formed the ministry in the state by winning 27 of the 30 seats, the CPI (M) won 2 and the CPI won 1 seat.

During the elections in 1972[13] the Indian National Congress (INC) bagged 41 seats with 44.83% of the vote share,[14] the CPM with 39.66% of the vote share secured 16 seats, the CPI got 1 seat with 16.09% of the vote share and Independents with 16.24% secured 2 seats. During these elections the tribal dominated *Tripura Upajati Samiti* received only 7.44% of the vote share and secured no seats.

In the elections to the state assembly in 1977, the CPM won 51 of the 60 seats with a vote share of 47%; the All India Forward Bloc (FBL) won 1 seat; the Revolutionary Socialist Party won 2 seats, the *Tripura Upajati Juba Samiti* (TUS) won 4 seats and the Independents won the remaining 2 seats with 7.93% of the votes polled. The INC could not secure any seat during these elections.[15]

In the 1983 elections to the state assembly the CPM won 37 seats with 46% of the vote share, while the INC won 12 with 40.73% of the votes. The Tribal political formation the TUS, which was becoming considerably formidable in electoral politics, secured 6 seats with 44.79% of the votes; the RSP secured 2 seats and the Independents won 3 seats. The rising fortune of the TUS was reflected also during the 1988 elections to the assembly during which the TUS secured 7 seats with 46.13% of the votes. The INC secured 25 seats, the CPM secured 25 while the RSP secured 2 seats. During the 1993 elections the CPM secured 44 seats of the 51 it contested with 44.78% of the vote share, while the INC secured only 10 seats of the 46 contested with 32.73% of the vote share. The TUS however, managed to secure only 1 seat with only 7.52%

of the popular votes. The RSP secured 2 seats, the FBL secured 1 seat and IND managed 1 seat from the remaining 4 seats with 1.58%, 0.80% and 6.16% of the popular votes respectively.

In 1998, CPM won 38 seats with 45.49% of the popular votes, the CPI won 1 seat with 1.38% of the votes, the INC won 13 seats with 33.96% of the votes share, the RSP won 2 seats with 1.65% of the votes and the remaining 4 seats were secured by the TUJS with 7.19% of the vote share. It may be worthwhile to note that the declining fortunes of the TUJS in electoral politics since 1993 might have been due to the decreasing support for electoral democracy by a majority of the tribal population who by now were strongly organised around insurgent groups seeking self-determination as the only means to achieve political power in the state. Moreover, the Congress was becoming a weak force primarily due to the fact that it was seen as a supporter of tribal insurgency and its alliance with the TUJS and surrendered TNV (Tripura National Volunteers) was not taken positively by the dominant ethnic group in the state.

Elections 2003: Ethnic Divisions and Electoral Outcomes

Since the beginning of fratricidal conflicts in the state unleashed by the various ethnic insurgent groups in the state, expression of the democratic franchise had been more often a blood-spilling exercise. However, despite all anticipations, unlike previous polls, the 2003 assembly elections in Tripura not only passed off, by and large peacefully but also sent a message that people of the state are tired of bloodshed and violence. Beleaguered by chronic militancy problem and protracted ethnic violence since the eighties Tripura has passed through two decades of blood and pain. Quite expectedly, when under the palpable shadow of militants' gun, Tripura inexorably went to polls on February 26, 2003 the key issue was "Peace and Harmony". Though the main question that is said to have determined the fate of the two political combines — ruling left and the opposition alliance of the Congress-I and the Indigenous Nationalist Party of Tripura (INPT) — was, which political formation would be able to provide peace, the ethnic base and traditional loyalties of both the combines ultimately decided the electoral outcome.

There was, no doubt, a strong anti-incumbency factor against the ruling Left Front, exacerbated by a critical unemployment problem and displacement of a large number of people from the interiors of the state. But the ruling front could make its high pitch poll campaign convincingly straight and loud: 'Pakistani ISI backed militants operating from Bangladesh is attempting to capture state power through its political front — the INPT'.

The bottom line of the message was clear: If the Congress-INPT comes to power, the very existence of the Bengalis will be at stake and all development funds for the interior areas dominated by the tribal communities will be siphoned by the tribal militants. This campaign by the ruling Left is rather an acknowledgement of the power of ethnic politics in electoral outcomes and given the fact that the *Janamangal Samiti* which was a precursor of left politics in the state began with a strong tribal base,[16] this campaign reflected the shift in the left political strategy. Impelled by the changing demographic profile and clear polarisation of electoral politics along ethnic lines in the state the left combine had to be guided more by pragmatic political considerations rather than by a coherent ideological programme.

The opposition attempted to counter the campaign saying that the Left Front in the wake of erosion of its traditional tribal base was playing the "Bengali card" but as is reflected in the election results this campaign did not make much impact. Evidently, the Left Front succeeded in its campaign and both the Bengali and the tribal electors rejected the Congress and its electoral partner INPT, giving them only 19 seats out of total 60. Congress got 13 out of 42 seats in its share while INPT had to be satisfied with only 6 out of 18 ST reserved constituencies. The Left Front got 41 seats with dominant partner CPM alone coming out with 38 MLAs, the RSP secured 2 seats and the CPI secured 1 seat.

Out of 19.33 lakh strong electorate about 79 percent cast their vote in the year 2003. Among them, 51.19 percent electors voted for Left Front and 45 percent for the Congress-INPT combine. In 1998 the left front had polled 49.11 percent votes — only 5.83 percent more than the votes together polled by Congress-Tripura Upajati Juba Samity and Tripura National Volunteers combine. The BJP, which had put up candidates for all the 60 candidates, had got 5.84 percent votes in its kitty in 1998. This year it got only 0.45 percent votes with no seats.

In a sense the poll verdict was not at all surprising. Congress in Tripura virtually does not have any tribal base and, in fact the hill people of Tripura have not been consistent in patronising any all-India party.[17] However, it was only in 1972 that Congress got the highest: 42 percent votes from the tribal areas. Since then it had to depend totally on a tribal party to sail through the elections. Even the Tribal Cell chairman of the Congress Kashiram Reang had to contest elections from a general seat.

During 1998 assembly elections the Congress had forged alliance with tribal fronts like Tripura Upajati Juba Samity (TUJS) and Tripura National Volunteers (TNV), which had joined mainstream following a peace agreement in 1988. But during the last five years, particularly after the Tripura Tribal Area Autonomous District Council elections in the April–May 2000, state politics underwent a dramatic change. Not only was there a new realignment of tribal forces but also the banned militant outfits started taking special interest in state politics directly offering armed support to tribal parties.[18]

Therefore, when the Tripura Tribal Areas Autonomous District Council (TTAADC) went to polls on April 30 and May 3, 2000, the banned National Liberation Front of Tripura militants working in favour of Indigenous People's Front of Tripura (IPFT), a breakaway group of the TUJS, unleashed an unprecedented terror campaign on the ruling CPM activists. NLFT cadres either killed or kidnapped CPM leaders, candidates and their close relatives. The situation was so volatile that even the TUJS, a strong political force in the tribal dominated hilly interior since 1967, was at the receiving end, had decided to boycott the ADC polls. The ruling Left Front government failed to grasp the gravity of the situation and could not counter the militants' terror tactics despite being in the power. The IPFT came to rule the autonomous district councils.

The ADC elections paved the way for a significant political development in the hills with TUJS joining the hands with the IPFT to float the Indigenous Nationalist Party of Twipra (INPT), in February in 2002. Reportedly, the merger of the two parties took place at the instance of the NLFT militants, which wanted a single tribal party for the Borok[19] people. The former militant leader and ex-president of the TNV, Bijoy Kumar Hrangkhawl, who had already dissolved the organization and merged with the IPFT, became the president of the INPT.

Another banned organization, All Tripura Tiger Force (ATTF) that allegedly helped the CPM at local level in the past, was by the year 2000 a disintegrated force following serious leadership crisis and desertion of armed cadres who surrendered before the security forces. The ATTF was not in a position to influence politics and confined itself to conducting stray ambushes in some parts of the state. In the absence of its archrival ATTF, the NLFT extended its area of operations and kept on targeting CPM workers in the tribal areas. According to a conservative estimate since 1993 when the third Left Front came to power under Chief Ministership of late Dasarath Deb, till February this year NLFT killed more than 560 CPM workers and top-level tribal leaders. Several thousands had to flee their home under selective and sustained onslaught. As the Marxists lost their traditional bastion in the hills under terror campaign, the INPT came to fill up the political vacuum. Despite the fact that there had always been an undercurrent of discontent between the former TUJS faction represented by moderate tribal leaders of 1967 era and IPFT faction comprising Shillong educated younger generation known as 'hardliners', the party managed to maintain a semblance of unity all along. It was actually these hardliners who reportedly were maintaining close interactions with the NLFT.

When the state readied for the 9th assembly elections of 2003, Congress in absence of any other alternative in the tribal areas had to forge electoral tie up with the INPT. But evidently, the party failed to fathom the sentiment of the majority Bengali voters who bore the brunt of militancy for the last 20 years. Added to it while INPT hardliners mostly from its frontal organizations raised highly ethnically sensitive demands like 50 percent ST reservation in the assembly and change of state's nomenclature from "Tripura" to '*Twipra*" (Originally an NLFT demand), the Congress had either kept mum on the issues or, worse, supported the demands.

This did not go down well with the majority non-tribals and when the Left Front launched a sustained campaign that the 'anti-Bengali NLFT militants were bent to bring the Congress-INPT in power at gunpoint', the doom was cast.

What, however, actually proved singularly devastating for the opposition alliance is the controversial Geneva Speech of INPT president Bijoy Hrangkhawl. The INPT chief who is also an MLA in his speech in Working Group of Indigenous Population Convention in Geneva in July last year criticized the role of the Bengali intelligentsia during Tripura's merger with Indian Union in 1949 and supported the outlawed militants for "Self determination of the Tripura tribals". The speech, when reported in local dailies, became a highly sensational issue and put the INPT and allies Congress in an awkward position with calls for legal action against Hrangkhawl on charges of 'sedition'. Both the parties sought to dispel the confusion saying 'right to self determination' did not mean 'sedition' but the damage was already done. The speech was full of distorted history and twisted facts and almost all political parties and apolitical organizations demanded Hrangkhawl's arrest. Moreover, only recently there were the cases against three INPT leaders and ADC Executive Members who had allegedly sent 67 tribal youths and students to NLFT camps for training in urban terrorism. This also came for ready reference to those who believed Hrangkhawl was in fact playing second fiddle for the NLFT. There were reminders that Hrangkhawl after his surrender in 1988 even did not express any regret for the killing of Bengalis by his TNV in the early eighties.

For the Left Front the Geneva Speech turned out to be a strong political weapon against the Congress INPT alliance. The ruling combine did not waste time to make it a major election issue to take away the wind from the opposition's sail. Congress-INPT also made some suicidal mistakes. The alliance antagonized the entire civil and police administrations and also the 9000 strong elite striking force, Tripura State Rifles (TSR), which is reputed for their skills in counter insurgency operation. The opposition launched a tirade against some of the top brass of the administration and the TSR in general accusing them of acting in a partisan manner favouring the Left Front. In the wake of opposition's allegations, the Election Commission debarred the Tripura State Rifles and also removed some officers including Joint Chief Election Officer and IGP law and order, from poll related duties. The EC decisions turned out to be blessing in disguise for the government. The experience during the ADC elections helped and the Left Front government deployed the entire TSR force in strategic locations for counter insurgency operations and plugged the traditional route of the militants in the deep interiors. It is suggested that New Delhi also indirectly helped the Tripura government to a great extent by sending more than 55,000 Central Para Military Forces to throw a security blanket in entire state that restricted the movement of the tribal insurgents to influence the electoral outcome.

Since the election was announced on January 11, the militants killed more than 18 persons. The bloodiest massacre was committed on Republic Day night at Mandaichoumuhani hamlet in West District where 11 CPM supporters were shot dead by the NLFT and their collaborators. But from February second week the CRPF started fanning out across the state. The BSF sealed the Indo-Bangla border to prevent intrusion bid of the militants from Bangladesh hideouts and the artillery regiments of the army began pro-active flush out campaign in the disturbed areas. Result was evident. NLFT attacks were reduced drastically as the armed guerrillas could not enter the tribal villages to sway the election results at gunpoint, arguably in favour of the Congress ally INPT. The February 26 elections were largely a peaceful affair barring some incidents in isolation. Since there were adequate security arrangements and militants were not around, the electors could exercise their franchise freely. The Congress INPT alliance took the high turn out everywhere as an indication of change in the guard. But as the results were announced on March 1, it was clear that majority Bengalis left Congress in general seats and the tribals rejected the INPT in the reserved Scheduled Tribe seats. Clearly, in both the case it was the alleged involvement of the NLFT militants, which cost dear to the opposition. Chief Minister Manik Sarkar and his party colleagues reasoned that fed up with the militancy the electors voted for peace. And the tribals in particular avenged the terror campaign during ADC elections when they were forced to vote at the direction of the armed militants.

That the 2003 Tripura polls were sharply polarized is evident from the fact that none of the other opposition parties like, NCP, Lok Jana Shakti and BJP led Tripura Ganatantrik Aikyo Mancha, which included Trinamul Congress, Janata Dal (United), Amara Bangali (a political formation of the Ananda Marga), Pashchadpada Gana Mancha (a platform of the OBC), could not make their presence felt. There were altogether 254 candidates and out of them 134 candidates including BJP president Ronojoy Deb, Trinamul Congress president Amal Mallik and Lok Jana Shakti president Papri Haldar forfeited their security.

Keeping in mind that people's mandate was for peace, minutes after the swearing in ceremony Chief Minister Manik Sarkar called upon the militants to eschew violence. "They can even hold peace talks with the central government directly and we do not have any opposition. Only precondition is that the talks must be held within the provisions of Indian Constitution", the Chief Minister said. He also offered all help to organizations and individuals who would be ready to mediate between the government and the militants. Sarkar's announcement was followed by a formal cabinet decision in this regard.

In conclusion we may say that the editorial warning of the Statesman of April 3, 1972 of an "explosive northeast"[20] has become ominous not only for most states of the region but especially for the then nascent state of Tripura that has been caught in a vortex of ethnic conflict and armed violence and holds true even today. The politicisation of ethnic identities impelled by sociological and economic imperatives has found new expressions and methods of institutionalisation that has the possibility of further fracturing the fragile ethnic relations and severely restricting the emergence of a democratic consensus on the conflicting values and claims. However, as some scholars perceive it, the participation of a large section of the population in electoral politics through democratic methods has the potential of negating secessionist violence and consolidating commitment to democracy.[21]

NOTES AND REFERENCES

1. Ranjit Kumar De, *Socio-Political Movements in India,* Mittal Publications, N. Delhi, 1998, p. 12.
2. See. www.nenanews.com. "Militants step up violence on poll eve in Tripura", Apr. 22–May 6, 2000.
3. See S.K. Chaube, *Hill Politics in Northeast India,* Orient Longman Ltd., Hyderabad, 1999, p. 213.
4. See Mahadev Chakraborty, "Autonomy Movements & National Integration: The Case of Tripura — A thematic approach", Seminar Paper for the Dept. of History, Tripura University. Feb 15, 1992.
5. See De, *op. cit.* 1998, p. 153.
6. See Chaube, *op. cit.* 1999, p. 204.
7. *Ibid.,* p. 207.
8. *Ibid.,* p. 214.
9. See Chaube. *op. cit.* 1985, p. 174.
10. Chaube *loc. cit.*
11. *Ibid.,* p. 176.
12. *Ibid.,* p. 176.
13. Prior to 1963, elections were being held for the 2 Lok Sabha seats and the 30 seats to the territorial council. The Tripura Territorial Council was converted into an Assembly on July 1, 1963. The strength of the state assembly was increased following the 1972 state reorganisation. See. S.K. Chaube, *Electoral Politics in Northeast India* (Universities Press, Madras, 1985), p. 173.

14. This refers to the vote share in terms of the seats contested and not the total percentage of votes polled. See http://www.eci.gov.in/archive/se72/StatReport_TP_72.pdf.
15. See Election Commission of India — State Election, 1977 to the Legislative Assembly of Tripura. *http://www.eci.gov.in/infoeci/key_stat/keystat_fs.htm.*
16. See De, *op. cit.*, 1998, p. 178.
17. See Chaube. *op. cit.*, 1999, p. 208.
18. See, www.nenanews.com *op. cit.* 2000.
19. A term the tribal people assign to themselves as an indigenous reference.
20. Cited by Chaube. *op. cit.* 1999, p. 233.
21. *Ibid.*, p. 251.

Electoral Politics in Manipur: A Study

Bhagat Oinam

The most appropriate highlight Manipur can have in the electoral map of India is that it was the first state (then a kingdom) to have exercised adult franchise after the colonial rule ended in the sub-continent. When rest of the country was yet to taste the fruits of liberal democracy, election based on adult franchise, the state had it as early as 1948 under the then constitution of the kingdom. This is with the effect that Manipur became independent from the British on 14 August 1947. And like many other princely kingdoms of Hyderabad and Kashmir, it began exercising its own sovereign administrative machineries till becoming part of India in 1949.

However, the equation has drastically changed in the last few decades. It is intriguing to see that the electoral history, which Manipur had, does not seem to cast any impression on its present state of affairs. It is currently facing a state of total crisis as close to anarchy, dwindled with confusion and lack of direction. Perhaps, no other state in the country has ever witnessed such unstable political climate as that of Manipur. Change of party loyalty, shifting alliances both at the individual and collective levels, are so frequent and ruthless that the state is now almost equated with the term 'instable' in the parlance of electoral politics. It may sound a bit of an exaggeration to begin with, but as one goes through the figures that are being shown in the Tables below, a clearer picture about the present state of affair will emerge. The deteriorating political values only reflect the state of alienation and lack of direction that the people and the society at large are faced with. Lack of social commitment and narrow individual aspirations are the highlights. Electoral behaviour both of the electorates as well as that of the elected representatives is one of the most apparent manifestations of this deep-seated crisis.

The manifestation of the crisis in terms of elaborate instances are the loss of party base, rise of money, muscle powers and 'gun culture', individual cult (paradoxically based on the legitimacy of the 'corrupt' and 'affluent'), loss of ideologies and values, and above all indifference of the electorates.

The instability in the political set up, a stark negative face of electoral democracy; has direct bearing on the governance. Where basic micro issues of governance are left unattended, the problems over a period of time have compounded making it an uphill task for the government in power to address to those problems. But the question is not of 'who' or 'which government of the past' have done the wrong. The issue is of 'the problems' that have slowly spread their tentacles and started eating up the very *élan vital* of the society. The problems that have turned much more complex are those that have emerged at the macro level, like those of 'merger to Indian dominion', 'proposed formation of Nagalim', etc. Though it may be incorrect to trace the ground for these macro issues to governance alone, but certainly governance is one of the major factors in the escalation of these macro issues. Due to lack of stable government and corresponding political will problems are going out of proportion. The causal factor of the crises lies invariably in political instability, which is currently visible. The state of fluidity is not too recent a phenomenon. It has its own history to look back; perhaps a retrospect may help understand the phenomenon better.

Ever since Manipur became a full-fledged state in 1972, after it was merged to the Indian dominion as a part-C state and subsequently made into a union territory in 1961, the state has witnessed as many as nine chief ministers with a frequency of change of guards on nineteen occasions. (This count is of post-statehood period.) On these counts is included President's rule with its seven alternate faces. Out of these seven times President's rule, at three counts, it culminated into assembly elections. This clearly shows not only the kind of political instability the state has been experiencing over the years but also the extent of interference of the power at the centre in the administration of the state (Table 1). This, of course, has been a trend rather than an exception in the entire country. Unfortunate tale has been that the Congress government at the centre had been hostile towards the state

Table 1: Chief Ministers and Governments since 1972

No.	*Chief Ministers*	*Governments*	*Period*	*Remarks*
1.	Md. Alimuddin	MPP led ULP Ministry	20.03.1972–28.03.1973	1st Legislative Assembly
		President's Rule	28.03.1973–04.03.1974	
2.	Md. Alimuddin	MPP led ULP Ministry	04.03.1974–10.07.1974	2nd Legislative Assembly
3.	Yangmaso Shaiza	PDF Ministry	10.07.1974–06.12.1974	
4.	R.K. Dorendro Singh	DLP Ministry	06.12.1974–23.07.1975	
5.	R.K. Dorendro Singh	Congress-CPI Ministry	23.07.1975–15.05.1977	Emergency
		President's Rule	15.05.1977–29.06.1977	
6.	Yangmaso Shaiza	Janata Party Ministry	29.06.1977–14.11.1979	
		President's Rule	14.11.1979–14.01.1980	
7.	R.K. Dorendro Singh	Congress-MPP Ministry	14.01.1980–27.11.1980	3rd Legislative Assembly
8.	Rishang Keishing	Congress Ministry	27.11.1980–28.02.1981	
		President's Rule	28.02.1981–19.06.1981	
9.	Rishang Keishing	Congress Ministry	19.06.1981–04.01.1985	
10.	Rishang Keishing	Congress Ministry	04.01.1985–04.03.1988	4th Legislative Assembly
11.	R.K. Jaichandra Singh	Congress Ministry	04.03.1988–23.02.1990	
12.	R.K. Ranbir Singh	ULF Ministry	23.02.1990–07.01.1992	5th Legislative Assembly
		President's Rule	07.01.1992–08.04.1992	
13.	R.K. Dorendro Singh	Congress Ministry	08.04.1992–31.12.1993	Dismissed on charges of bad law and order
		President's Rule	31.12.1993–13.12.1994	
14.	Rishang Keishing	Congress Ministry	13.12.1994–24.02.1995	
15.	Rishang Keishing	Congress Ministry	24.02.1995–16.12.1997	6th Legislative Assembly
16.	W. Nipamacha Singh	MSCP led United Front Ministry	16.12.1997–02.03.2000	Split in Congress
17.	W. Nipamacha Singh	MSCP led United Front Ministry	02.03.2000–14.02.2001	7th Legislative Assembly
18.	Radhabinod Koijam	Samata led MDF Ministry	15.02.2001–02.06.2001	Assembly under animated
		President's Rule	02.06.2001–07.03.2002	suspension was later dismissed on 07.09.2001
19.	O. Ibobi Singh	Congress led SPF Ministry	07.03.2002–06.05.2003	8th Legislative Assembly

Source: Manipur Information Centre, New Delhi.

governments ruled by non-Congress parties. Non-Congress governments were seen as seed for possible emergence of regional powers (and possible disintegration of the country), be it CPI (M) or Janata Party, not to mention DMK, National Conference or Manipur Peoples' Party (MPP). Reference can be made to Kashmir where Nehru unceremoniously toppled the then National Conference government of Sheikh Abdullah in 1953 without providing justifiable reasons. The only reason, if any, was the fear of loosing Kashmir as an independent Muslim country. The other instance was the pulling down of DMK government at Tamil Nadu in January 1975 by instigating defection. This drama of President's rule reached its height in 1980s when 9 non-Congress governments were simply toppled by bringing in President's rule. Even though such instances were substantive in number, subtle difference could still be made with regards to the northeastern states. In fact, the smaller states of northeast have been more vulnerable to such onslaughts of the centre. Justifications for such acts are provided by linking them to the unity and integrity of the country, with these states being shown as 'all time sensitive'. President's rule was only one of the facets of the hegemonic control of the central government. There had been several cases where a non-Congress government was toppled and a new government installed by instigating defection and horse-trading. The events that were witnessed in Manipur in its post-statehood days can serve as a paradigm case. The first state government headed by MPP after Manipur got statehood, which came into existence in 1972 as manifestation of regional aspiration of the people of the state, was summarily pulled down instigating defection and horse-trading. A crisis created in number game culminated in the so-called 'inevitable' President's rule leading to holding of the second assembly election within a span of two years. The whole episode reached its climax when the MPP government that came back to power in the second assembly election was again pulled down within a span of four months. It was a sheer show of strength of an ever unaccountable, and all-powerful, Central government. Ironically, perhaps, it was to uphold the constitutional legitimacy of unitary structure as against federalism. The readily available argument with the centre was that the political goals of these regional parties, say about 'autonomy', will in the long run head towards disintegration of the country. Perhaps this perception, associated with an underlying fear, in the given point of time was based on some genuine conditions — that India as an imagined nation state was just being conceived after several initial set backs that includes the creation of Pakistan.

It is now that India has entered fifty-sixth year of independence. Not only the country has witnessed fall of Congress at the centre in a number of occasions, but also the emergence of regional parties in the coalition politics. And the country still goes strong defying all speculations and fear. The perception that emergence of regional parties in the peripheral states is a threat to country's integrity has been proved wrong over these decades. Contrarily the regional parties are able to attend to the aspirations of the people much better than their so-called 'national' counter part.[1] Concentration of power in the country's capital has already been shown as one of the many reasons of disenchantment over regional neglect and imbalances. In the long run, centre's interference has turned out to be more harmful for the country in the successful exercise of liberal electoral procedures. Keeping aside the question on the merits and demerits of regional aspirations, what turns out to be a blunder is the means employed by the power brokers at the centre to destabilise the state governments. A trend has already been set where money and muscle powers can lure and enforce change in the power equations. And the game of defection is learnt fast by the local representatives. Over a period of few decades the disease has percolated to almost all sections of the electorates.

Demographic Composition

Perhaps highlighting the demographic composition of the state will show the complexity in electoral equations that exist among communities and tribes. Electoral behaviour is by and large determined by these relationships. Of course, individual MLA's narrow political aspirations is an additional factor which instead of having relationship with demography bear imprints of centre's shifting game of power and money as mentioned earlier. Much of the instability and fluidity in terms of post-electoral equation among the MLAs on government formation are governed by these factors.

Manipur with its area of 22,327 sq km has a population of 23,88,634 (2001 census). There are 60 electoral constituencies, of which 19 are reserved for ST and 1 for SC. The constituencies are spread over nine districts, viz. Imphal East, Imphal West, Thoubal, Bishnupur, Ukhrul, Senapati, Tamenglong, Churachandpur and Chandel. Out of these, first four are in the valley and the other five are in hills. Majority of the constituencies (numbering 40) is spread over the 4 districts of the valley and rest in the 5 hill districts. For the parliamentary election, there are two constituencies — Inner Manipur and Outer Manipur. Total number of electorates as recorded in the last (seventh) assembly election was 14,15,895 (6,81,687 in the valley and 7,34,208 in the hills).

The population of the state can be broadly divided into highlanders and lowlanders. The former consists of almost exclusively the scheduled tribe population (very loosely grouped recently into Nagas and Kukis) whereas the latter consist of mainly the Meiteis and other communities such as the Meitei Pangals (Manipuri Muslims). The Meiteis (Hindu and Sanamahi[2]) with a population of 13.62 lakhs constitutes the majority community. The Meitei Pangals (Manipuri Muslims) has a population of 1.67 lakhs. Total tribal population is 7.13 lakhs. Others (Nepalis and *Mayangs*[3]) have a population of 1.46 lakhs.[4]

Most of the population of the state is concentrated in the valley, which comprises of almost all ethnic communities and other non-Manipuris (*mayangs*). Majority of the inhabitants in the valley are Meiteis who can be divided into 3 sections based on religious practices; Meitei Hindus, Meitei Sanamahi, and Meitei Muslims. This classification however may be merged into two when criterion of a loose electoral behaviour is brought into focus, i.e. between the Meitei Muslims and general Meiteis. However, by and large, the electoral politics is free from the communal virus that affects the rest of the country. This is in spite of a possible trend among the Muslims in a couple of constituencies where they constitute a sizable population (Mayang Imphal and Lilong), to vote in general for Muslim candidates. For the Meiteis, voting pattern is not based on whatever religious divide that exist among them (such as Meitei Hindu and Meitei Sanamahi). This is mainly because the division between Meitei Hindus and Meitei Sanamahis, though based on the differences in the religious practices, both are but one cultural unit. Imbibing of Vaisnavism has not brought any division in the cultural life of the Meiteis. Rather, a strong system of clan lineage and its cultural practices have retained them (both the followers of Sanamahi and Vaisnavism) as one socio-cultural unit. Voting behaviour among the Meiteis to some extent is influenced by this clan lineage, more particularly in the rural constituencies.

Although voting is not done on religious grounds in the state, certain identity-based politics do occur, especially in the hills. The groupings based on tribe identity (as an extended form of clan identity) play a crucial role. This is all the more conspicuous since the infamous Kuki-Naga clash in the 90s. A divide among the Nagas and Kukis, to take a loose structure, is quite visible in the areas where distribution of population among these tribes is more or less even. This is also visible in all those areas where sizable number of population of any of these tribes exists. In the valley, to some extent, clan lineage plays a crucial role. This may be because of the fact that the valley population is more or less homogeneous. Meiteis across the state (Meitei Pangals included) belongs to one cultural group speaking the same language with little variations in dialects.

Formation of group cluster as structurally or ideologically different, if not opposed, from one another has been the basis of the very practice of electoral democracy. The grouping goes to clan or caste lineages (hereditary or social givenness) of Indian experience, which applies very well in the case of Manipur. The grouping based on heredity and social givenness, with little variations, may be seen as a unique experience of the developing and underdeveloped countries where practice of electoral democracy is through an imported package than indigenously internalised. There are tendencies where people of a clan demographically distributed in cluster (particularly in rural areas) tend to vote for a candidate close to their kin. Feudal ethos still operate strongly. There are also instances where a village as a whole or a *leikai* (*mohallah* in a loose sense) tends to go for collective voting. No caste-based electoral behaviour however is witnessed among the (general) Meiteis. This is mainly because the Hindu caste structure (among the Meiteis, there are Brahmins — locally known as *Bamons*, the Kshatriyas, and the scheduled caste) not only has a different historicity in the state but it does not affect the Meiteis as a unified cultural entity in the state. Though the Kshatriya population forms an overwhelming majority, for almost whole of the Meitei population barring those in the schedule caste areas of

Kakching, Sekmai, etc. was converted into Kshatriya fold (through sanskritisation, to use a loose category), to demarcate and create caste-based electoral constituencies in the state cannot be thought of *Bamons*, who are the migrants from the mainland India and carriers of Vaisnavism in the state, forms a small part of the valley population and so far has not made any mark in the electoral politics. Though clustering in terms of aligning to any particular candidate is generally formed, it has been either clan-based or area-based. Grouping in terms of religious divide has not come out in large scale in the state, both in the valley as well as in the hills.[5]

In the hills, there are as many as thirty-two tribes with varying population-strength, starting from Thadou, Tangkhul and Mao, to Moyon, Monsang and Thangal, falling within the comparatively new political constructs. These constructs that can better be seen as ethno-political[6] are the Naga, Kuki, and Zeliangrong. While division and exclusivity between Naga and Kuki is near total[7] both ethnically as well as ideologically, the third ethno-political group, Zeliangrong, has a unique status. Some of the tribes under Zeliangrong prefer to be under the Naga confederation subsuming Zeliangrong movement under a pan-Naga banner. There are also other tribes who do not fall into any of these new categories. Tribes such as Simte, Paite, Mate, Kom, Tedimchin, Vaiphei, etc. do not wish to be put under any of these ethno-political categories. A new name under Zomi encompasses these tribes giving themselves a distinctive identity from the Kukis.

Interesting feature in the hills is the demographic distributions in the five districts marked by different combination of the above-mentioned tribes with different identities. Where districts like Tamenglong and Ukhrul are clearly dominated by Zeliangrongs and Tangkhul Nagas respectively, Kuki and other ethnically closer tribes like Zomi, Mizo, Hmar, etc. dominate Churachandpur district. Two other hill districts, Senapati and Chandel, are areas of contention between the Nagas and the Kukis. However, Nagas seem to have more influence in these two districts, especially in terms of both demographic distribution and arms strength of their insurgent organizations. The decade long Naga-Kuki conflict has shown the involvement of insurgent organisations (primarily formed on ethnic line) in the inter-ethnic conflict. This has not only escalated the quantum of violence but also made the conflict more decisive. The amount of causalities that the civilians have faced at both ends, the impression of which have entered in the collective psyche of these tribes in the form of intense hatred, will take a long time to heal. Though 'peace' is the current password, violence can spread in any form at any moment. Violence only starts in stray isolated incidents, which is quickly channelised through an already existing ideological construct through sloganeering or spreading rumour. Several other methods are employed. This divide marked by hatred at the micro level does exert a major impact in the voting behaviour of the electorates, not only in the areas where conflict took place but also to those areas where both the conflicting tribes co-exist. It is temporarily homogenising[8] because to an otherwise scattered people in cluster that essence of ethnic exclusivity and conflict is passed on. This phenomenon in a softer form was witnessed in the recent agitation against the construction of Tipaimukh dam in the state by the Naga civil societies.[9] Though several arguments based on environmental hazards were cited, barring a few Meiteis in the civil society groups, among others, the debate ('conflict' to be an apt word) is largely guided by ethnic interests. The issue no more remains between the 'affected' and the 'beneficiaries'. Similar instance is the tussle among the MLAs during the initiation of the proposed creation of a separate district of Kangpokpi. The proposed district dominated by the Kukis has been strongly opposed by the Naga lobby.[10] This has also been one of the major factors for the Naga-Kuki conflict.

These ethnic equations rather than party considerations are determining factors in the voting behaviour. The complexity of ethnic relation can be witnessed in most of the hill districts barring the Ukhrul district, which is predominantly inhabited by Tangkhul Nagas. Equation is not only at the level of inter ethnic-community but also at that of intra ethnic-community. I am making a distinction between 'tribe' and 'ethnic community' for functional purposes, the former referring to those traditionally existing groups having the same dialect and cultural practices, and the latter to a configuration of several of those tribes attempting to create a common language and cultural practices. Ethnic community is a politicised entity, a developed stage of a tribe or tribes, but at the same time about the constituent members trying to become a new tribe. In other words, the movement from tribe to ethnic community is a process of identity formation by the constituent members. It is a process of internalising a new identity. The ethnic equations can be witnessed not only between two ethnic communities, say Nagas and Kukis, but also among constituent tribes within the Kuki or Naga configurations. Electoral contests in the constituencies of Nungba and Churachandpur, for instance, were precisely on this line — former among the tribes within the Zeliangrong Nagas and latter within the Kuki-Chin-Mizo group.

Stable Instability: Individual and Shifting Party Loyalty

Instability can be witnessed in the inter-party alliances and shifting party loyalty of the individual MLAs. Nature of party alliances is fluid and based on several considerations. With lack of absolute majority for any party in the last few assembly elections, formation of alliance among the 'like-minded parties' has become a natural phenomenon than exception. It is difficult to find a particular trend that explains these alliance partnerships. Sometimes it is by virtue of a party decision reflecting the alliance formation at the centre. And at times it is engineered by the pragmatic considerations of the MLAs. Often there have been cases where the entire MLAs of a party in defiance to party high command at the centre or the state merge with the ruling party or form a new party to merge with the ruling alliance. In all these forms of alliance formation the under current is the individual aspiration to be in the ruling side rather than in the opposition. Exception to such a trend is minimal with stray incidents of one opposition Congress MLA during the sixth state assembly and few MLAs of MPP earlier.

Both pre-poll and post-poll alliances operate with peculiar tendencies. Pre-poll electoral alliance in Manipur is not a clear form of alliance as the term implies. Though alliances are made under a makeshift banner. There were cases of 'friendly' contest among the alliance partners. Such a practice was first experienced in the state (and perhaps for the first time in the country) during the seventh assembly election (Table 2). Though MSCP and FPM aligned to form UFM, it was not an alliance in the true sense of the term. Both MSCP and FPM were in the fray in spite of forming UFM. Though it looked a rare affair then, such a practice is not any more uncommon today as similar practice was recently witnessed in the Nagaland assembly election, 2003. Though DAN was formed as a pre-poll front with the alliance of parties like BJP, SAP, etc. there were 'friendly contest' among the allies. The so-called 'friendly contest' often used now does have very little friendliness in the contest. Though justification for such an alliance is referred to incumbency factor (against the then ruling Congress government), it is more with the view to form alliance in the post-poll scenario that such a makeshift pre-poll alliance comes to existence. Such a practice only endorses to what may be called the 'stable instability' of alliances.

Table 2: Pre-poll Alliances of 7th Assembly Election

	Alliance-wise Parties and Others	No. of seats contested	Seats won	% of votes shared
	United Front of Manipur (UFM)			
1.	Manipur State Congress Party (MSCP)	57	23	26.28
2.	Federal Party of Manipur (FPM)	39	06	09.44
	Total		29	
	Secular Democratic Front (SDF)			
3.	Indian National Congress (INC)	47	10+1	18.31
4.	Manipur Peoples Party (MPP)	29	04	07.90
5.	Communist Party of India (CPI)	15	–	03.60
6.	Communist Party of India (Marxist) (CPM)	04	–	0.30
7.	Janata Dal (Secular) [JD(S)]	08	01	1.58
8.	Revolutionary Socialist Party (RSP)	03	–	0.08
	Total		16	
	Manipur Democratic Alliance (MDA)			
9.	Bharatiya Janata Party (BJP)	39	06	11.28
10.	Samata Party (SAP)	36	01	06.68
11.	Kuki National Assembly (KNA)	01	–	00.06
12.	Janata Dal (United) [JD(U)]	18	01	01.79
	Total		08	
	Others			
13.	National Congress Party (NCP)	41	04+1	07.87
14.	Rashtriya Janata Dal (RJD)	15	01	01.83
15.	National Peoples Party (NPP)	01	–	–
16.	Independents	48	01	03.00
	Grand Total	402	60	100

Source: Manipur Information Centre, New Delhi.

As much as one finds fluidity in such alliances, individual loyalty to party is equally an unpredictable affair. Though shifting party loyalty had been a normal practice (Table 4) in the state, it reached its height during the period from 2000 to 2002 (Table 3).

Table 3: Shifting of Party Loyalty

	Candidate	Constituency	Feb. 2000	March 2000	Feb. 2001	May 2001
1.	K. Tomba Singh	Khundrakpam	MPP	MSCP	BJP	BJP
2.	W. Thoiba Singh	Heingang	FPM	FPM	BJP	BJP
3.	N. Bihari Singh	Khurai	MSCP	MSCP	BJP	BJP
4.	Vivekraj Wangkhem	Khetrigao	–	–	–	SAP
5.	S. Dhananjoy Singh	Thongju	MSCP	MSCP	MSCP	MSCP
6.	H. Bidur Singh	Keirao	MSCP	MSCP	BJP	BJP
7.	S. Chandro Singh	Andro	MPP	MSCP	BJP	BJP
8.	Ksh. Biren Singh	Lamlai	MSCP	MSCP	BJP	BJP
9.	Radhabinod Koijam	Thangmeiband	INC	INC	SAP	SAP
10.	P. Achou Singh	Uripok	MSCP	MSCP	BJP	BJP
11.	Kh. Loken Singh	Sagolband	JD (S)	JD (S)	JD (L)	JD (L)
12.	L. Jayantakumar	Keisamthong	–	FPM	SAP	SAP
13.	H. Bhubon Singh	Singjamei	BJP	BJP	BJP	BJP
14.	R.K. Dorendra Singh	Yaiskul	BJP	BJP	BJP	BJP
15.	H. Borobabu Singh	Wangkhei	BJP	BJP	BJP	BJP
16.	Kh. Chandra Singh	Sekmai (SC)	BJP	BJP	BJP	BJP
17.	S. Rajen Singh	Lamsang	MSCP	MSCP	MSCP	MSCP
18.	H. Lokhon Singh	Konthoujam	MSCP	MSCP	MSCP	MSCP
19.	L. Chandramani Singh	Patsoi	MSCP	MSCP	MSCP	MSCP
20.	Okram Joy Singh	Langthabal	MPP	MPP	MPP	MPP
21.	W. Leima Devi	Naoriya Pakhanglakpa	IND	IND	IND	IND
22.	W. Nipamacha Singh	Wangoi	MSCP	MSCP	MSCP	MSCP
23.	Kh. Amutombi Singh	Mayang Imphal	INC	INC	SAP	SAP
24.	Th. Bira Singh	Nambol	MSCP	MSCP	MSCP	MSCP
25.	Y. Jiten Singh	Oinam	MSCP	MSCP	BJP	BJP
26.	K. Govindas Singh	Bishenpur	MSCP	MSCP	BJP	BJP
27.	L. Kerani Singh	Moirang	INC	INC	SAP	SAP
28.	H. Sanayaima Singh	Thanga	MSCP	MSCP	BJP	BJP
29.	S. Bira Singh	Kumbi	MSCP	MSCP	MSCP	MSCP
30.	Md. Alauddin	Lilong	NCP	MSCP	BJP	BJP
31.	L. Tomba Singh	Thoubal	MSCP	MSCP	BJP	BJP
32.	Nimaichand Luwang	Wangkhem	INC	INC	SAP	SAP
33.	M. Okendro Singh	Heirok	INC	INC	SAP	SAP
34.	M. Hemanta Singh	Wangjing Tentha	MSCP	MSCP	MSCP	MSCP
35.	L. Jatra Singh	Khangabok	MPP	MSCP	MSCP	MSCP
36.	M. Manihar Singh	Wabgai	INC	INC	SAP	SAP
37.	N. Nimai Singh	Kakching	INC	INC	SAP	SAP
38.	M. Kunjo Singh	Hiyanglam	MSCP	MSCP	BJP	BJP
39.	K. Ranjit Singh	Sugnoo	BJP	BJP	BJP	BJP
40.	A. Biren Singh	Jiribam	MSCP	MSCP	MSCP	MSCP
41.	Hangkhanpao	Chandel (ST)	RJD	MSCP	MSCP	MSCP
42.	Onjamang Haokip	Tengnoupal (ST)	NCP	MSCP	BJP	BJP
43.	Rishang Keishing	Phungyar (ST)	INC	INC	INC	INC
44.	D. Shaiza	Ukhrul (ST)	BJP	BJP	BJP	BJP

(contd.)

(contd. Table 3)

	Candidate	Constituency	Feb. 2000	March 2000	Feb. 2001	May 2001
45.	Khashim Ruivah	Chingai (ST)	FPM	FPM	FPM	FPM
46.	C. Doungel	Saikul (ST)	NCP	MSCP	BJP	BJP
47.	L. Jonathan	Karong (ST)	INC	INC	SAP	SAP
48.	M. Thohrii	Mao (ST)	INC	INC	SAP	SAP
49.	K. Raina	Tadubi (ST)	FPM	FPM	BJP	BJP
50.	Thangminlien Kipgen	Kangpokpi	NCP	MSCP	BJP	BJP
51.	Haokholet Kipgen	Saitu (ST)	FPM	FPM	SAP	SAP
52.	Mangaibou	Tamei (ST)	MSCP	MSCP	BJP	BJP
53.	Samuel Jendai	Tameglong (ST)	MSCP	MSCP	BJp	BJP
54.	Gangmumei Kamei	Nungba (ST)	FPM	FPM	FPM	FPM
55.	Ngursanglur	Tipaimuk (ST)	NCP	NCP	NCP	NCP
56.	Songchinkhup	Thanlon (ST)	MSCP	MSCP	BJP	BJP
57.	T. Manga Vaiphei	Henglep (ST)	INC	INC	SAP	SAP
58.	V. Hangkhanlian	Churachandpur (ST)	MSCP	MSCP	MSCP	MSCP
59.	M. Chungkhosei	Saikot (ST)	MSCP	MSCP	MSCP	MSCP
60.	N. Zatawn	Singhat (ST)	JD (U)	MSCP	MSCP	MSCP

Greed of the MLAs added by weak leadership created the menace Ultimate height of this 'shift' culminated in the holding of eighth state assembly election in February 2002, just two years after the seventh state assembly election was held. In addition to the data shown in Table 3, there had been many more informal shifts during the period from February 2001 to June 2001, which have not been recorded here (Table 3). With the June 18 uprising (2001) the expectation among the public was the 'end of horse trading and shifting of party.' This however has not happened. Just after the eighth state assembly election most of the MSCP MLAs in spite of being in the ruling alliance joined Congress. So had Samata part and NCP MLAs. Though the frequency and quantum of shift hav been lesser during the present period the practice itself seems t be something hard to part with.

As can be witnessed from Table 4, importance of party is to large extent downplayed by individual. Though political partie are equated with leadership as the case is in the entire countr the case of Manipur shows a different picture. It is not a questic of party being equated with the leadership but of party having r significance to the electorates. It is the individual who is all th matters. This phenomenon, however, is a later developmer Earlier, during '60s and '70s, parties like Congress, CPI and MI

Table 4: Winning Party and Candidate from 4th to 8th Assembly Election

Constituency	1985	1990	1995	2000	2002
1. Khundrakpam	IND L. Lala	MPP K. Benoy Singh	MPP K. Benoy Singh *By-election MSCP* L. Lala Singh	MPP K. Tomba Singh	SAP (now INC) L. Lala
2. Heingang	INC W. Jagor Singh	Cong. (S) W. Jagor Singh	FPM W. Thoiba Singh	FPM W. Thoiba Singh	DPP Nongthombam Biren
3. Khurai	IND Ng. Atomba	MPP Ch. Manihar Singh	IND N. Bihari Singh	MSCP N. Bihari Singh	FPM N. Bihari Singh
4. Khetrigao	INC Muhamuddin Shah	INC Muhamuddin Shah	JD W. Basanta Singh *Bi-elec.* MSCP Muhamuddin Shah	SAP Vivekraj Wangkhem	MSCP* Vivekraj Wangkhem
5. Thongju	IND N. Bisheshwar	Cong. (S) S. Braja-gopal Sharma	MPP S. Dhananjoy Singh	MSCP S. Dhananjoy Singh	MSCP (now INC) Bijoy Koijam
6. Keirao	INC Abdul Matalip	JD H. Bidur Singh	INC H. Bidur Singh	MSCP H. Bidur Singh	INC Md. Alauddin Khan
7. Andro	INC L. Amujao Singh	Congress (I) L. Amujao Singh	MPP S. Chandra Singh	MPP S. Chandra Singh	FPM S. Chandra Singh
8. Lamlai	INC Y. Kerani Singh	CPI Ph. Parijat	MPP Ksh. Biren Singh	MSCP Ksh. Biren Singh	CPI Ph. Parijat
9. Thangmeiband	INC Radhabinod Koijam	MPP Ng. Kumarjit Singh	INC Radhabinod Koijam	INC Radhabinod Koijam	BJP M. Bhorot Singh
10. Uripok	INC P. Achou Singh	INC T. Gunadhwaja Singh	MPP N. Nodiachand Singh	MSCP P. Achou Singh	INC L. Nandakumar Singh
11. Sagolband	IND Salam Damudor	INC R.K. Joychandra Singh	MPP M. Kumar Singh	JD (S) Kh. Loken Singh	MNC S. Natum Singh

(contd.)

(contd. Table 4)

Constituency	1985	1990	1995	2000	2002
12. Keisamthong	INC L. Lalit Singh	MPP R.K. Ranbir Singh	MPP R.K. Ranbir Singh	FPM L. Jayanta-kumar	FPM L. Ibomcha Singh
13. Singjamei	INC I. Tompok Singh	INC I. Hemo-chandra Singh	INC I. Hemo-chandra Singh	BJP H. Bhubon Singh	FPM I. Hemo-chandra Singh
14. Yaiskul	INC R.K. Dorendro Singh	INC R.K. Dorendro Singh	BJP E. Kunjeshwar Singh	BJP R.K. Dorendro Singh	BJP R.K. Dorendro Singh
15. Wangkheï	INC Irabot Yumkham	MPP H. Borobabu Singh	INC Irabot Yumkham	BJP H. Borobabu Singh	MSCP* Irabot Yumkham
16. Sekmai (SC)	INC Kh. Leirenjao Singh	INC N. Biren Singh	INC N. Biren Singh	BJP Kh. Chandra Singh	FPM Ningthoujam Biren
17. Lamsang	IND M. Deven Singh	MPP M. Deven Singh	INC S. Rajen Singh	MSCP S. Rajen Singh	INC W. Brajabidhu Singh
18. Konthoujam	INC H. Lokhon Singh	MPP H. Thoithoi Singh	INC H. Lakhon Singh	MSCP H. Lakhon Singh	DPP Dr. Th. Meinya
19. Patsoi	INC L. Chandra-mani Singh	Cong. (S) N. Ibomcha Singh	INC L. Chandra-mani Singh	MSCP L. Chandra-mani Singh	CPI M. Nabadwip
20. Langthabal	MPP O. Joy Singh	MPP O. Joy Singh	INC K. Babudhon Singh	MPP O. Joy Singh	MPP O. Joy Singh
21. Naoriya Pakhang-lakpa	INC W. Angou Singh	Congress (I) W. Angou Singh	IND Akoijam Lanngam	IND W. Leima Devi	INC W. Leima Devi
22. Wangoi	JP W. Nipamacha Singh	Cong. (S) W. Nipamacha Singh	INC W. Nipamacha Singh	MSCP W. Nipamacha Singh	MSCP (now INC) Y. Mani Singh
23. Mayang Imphal	JP M. Nilachandra Singh	JD Kh. Amutombi Singh	INC M. Nilachandra Singh	INC Kh. Amutombi Singh	FPMM. Nilachandra Singh
24. Nambol	INC Th. Chaoba Singh	Congress (I) Th. Chaoba Singh	MPP N. Loken Singh	MSCP Th. Bira Singh	INC N. Loken Singh

25. Oinam	INC K. Bira Singh	Congress (I) K. Apabi Devi	MPP Y. Jiten Singh	MSCP Y. Jiten Singh	NCP (now INC) L. Radhakishore Singh
26. Bishnupur	IND Th. Udhop Singh	JD Kh. Jibon Singh	INC K. Govindas Singh	MSCP K. Govindas Singh	MSCP (now INC) K. Govindas Singh
27. Moirang	JP M. Koireng Singh	Congress (I) M. Koireng Singh	MPP Md. Hesha-muddin	INC L. Kerani Singh	FPM S. Gopal Singh
28. Thanga	IND H. Sanayaima	MPP S. Ibohal	JD T. Mangibabu Singh	MSCP H. Sanayaima Singh	FPM S. Ibohal
29. Kumbi	IND S. Bira Singh	CPI N. Mangi Singh	CPI N. Mangi Singh	MSCP S. Bira Singh	CPI N. Mangi Singh
30. Lilong	MPP Alauddin	Congress (I) Helaluddin Khan	INC Helaluddin Khan	NCP Alauddin	INC Dr. Md. Maniruddin Shaikh
31. Thoubal	JP Leitanthem Tomba	JD Th. Krishna Singh	MPP Leitanthem Tomba	MSCP Leitanthem Tomba	FPM Leitanthem Tomba
32. Wangkhem	IND Dr. Nimai-chand Luwang	INC Dr. Nimai-chand Luwang	INC Dr. Nimai-chand Luwang	INC Dr. Nimai-chand Luwang	MPP Dr. Nimai-chand Luwang
33. Heirok	INC M. Ibotombi	JD N. Komol Singh	INC M. Okendro Singh	INC M. Okendro Singh	FPM N. Sovakiran Singh
34. Wangjing Tentha	CPI M. Nara Singh	CPI M. Nara Singh	INC M. Hemanta Singh	MSCP M. Hemanta Singh	CPI M. Nara Singh
35. Khangabok	IND O. Ibobi Singh	INC O. Ibobi Singh	MPP L. Jatra Singh	MPP L. Jatra Singh	INC O. Ibobi Singh
36. Wabagai	IND M. Manihar Singh	INC W. Manihar Singh	MPP Abdul Salam	INC M. Manihar Singh	INC Md. Abdul Salam
37. Kakching	IND Y. Thambal Singh	INC N. Nimai Singh	CPI Ksh. Irabot Singh	INC N. Nimai Singh	CPI Thokchom Tomba
38. Hiyanglam	INC E. Biramani Singh	INC E. Biramani Singh	JD M. Kunjo Singh	MSCP M. Kunjo Singh	NCP E. Biramani Singh
39. Sugnoo	INC M. Babu Singh	JD L. Ibomcha Singh	JD M. Babu Singh	BJP K. Ranjit	INC K. Ranjit

(contd.)

(contd. Table 4)

Constituency	1985	1990	1995	2000	2002
40. Jiribam	INC Th. Devendra	INC Th. Devendra	INC Th. Devendra	MSCP A. Biren Singh	INC Th. Devendra
41. Chandel (ST)	IND H.T. Thungam	JD B.T. Behring	JD Hangkhanpao	RJD Hangkhanpao	BJP B.D. Behring
42. Tengnoupal (ST)	IND J. Haokip	INC W. Morung Makunga	INC W. Morung Makunga	NCP Onjamang Haokip	SAP D.K. Korungthang
43. Phungyar (ST)	INC Rishang Keishing	INC Rishang Keishing	INC Rishang Keishing	INC Rishang Keishing	MSCP Wungnao-shang
44. Ukhrul (ST)	IND A.S. Arthur	JD Hangmila Shaiza	INC A.S. Arthur	BJP D. Shaiza	BJP D. Shaiza
45. Chingai (ST)	INC R.V. Mingthing	MPP Somi. A. Shimray	INC M. Horam	FPM Khasim Ruivah	INC A. Aza
46. Saikul (ST)	IND H. Khongsei	Cong. (S) C. Doungel	MPP C. Doungel	NCP C. Doungel	NCP C. Doungel
47. Karong (ST)	IND K.H. Benjamin Banee	INC K.H. Benjamin Banee	SP L. Jonathan	INC L. Jonathan	FPM P.S. Henry Paotei
48. Mao (ST)	INC Sosow Lorho	INC Sosow Lorho	Cong. (S) M. Thohrii	INC M. Thohrii	INC R.K. Thekho
49. Tadubi (ST)	INC Ng. Luikang	INC Ng. Luikang	JD O. Lohrii *Bi-elec.* MSCP Haokholet Kipgen	FPM K. Raina	INC Francis Ngajokpa
50. Kangpokpi	IND Kishore Thapa	JD L.S. John	MPP Thangminlien Kipgen	NCP Thangminlien Kipgen	FPM Thangminlien Kipgen
51. Saitu (ST)	INC S. Paokhosei	MPP Ngamthang Haokip	MPP Ngamthang Haokip	FPM Haokholet Kipgen	INC Ngamthang Haokip
52. Tamei (ST)	IND I.D. Dijunang	INC I.D. Dijunang	IND D.P. Panmei	MSCP Z. Mangaibou	INC Z. Mangaibou

53. Tamenglong (ST)	INC J. Panmei	JD Daisin Pamei	SP Samuel Jendai	MSCP Samuel Jendai	FPM Samuel Jendai
54. Nungba (ST)	INC Gaikhangam	INC Gaikhangam	FPM Gangmumei Kamei	FPM Gangmumei Kamei	INC Gaikhangam
55. Tipaimuk (ST)	IND Ngurdinglien	JD Selkai Hrangchal	INC Dr. Chaltonlien	NCP Ngusanglur	INC Dr. Chaltonlien
56. Thanlon (ST)	INC T. Phungjathang	INC T. Phungjathang	MPP Songchinkhup	MSCP Songchinkhup	INC Songchinkhup
57. Henglep (ST)	IND Sehpu	Cong. (S) Holkhomang Haokip	JD Sehpu Haokip *Bi-elec.* FPM Thangjalam Haokip	INC T. Manga Vaiphei	SAP T. Manga Vaiphei
58. Churachandpur (ST)	KNA Rothangliana	NPP V. Hangkhanlian	NPP V. Hangkhanlian	MSCP V. Hangkhanlian	INC T. Phungjathang
59. Saikot (ST)	MPP Ngulkhohau	KNA T.N. Haokip	MPP T.N. Haokip	MSCP M. Chungkhosei	INC T.N. Haokip
60. Singhat (ST)	INC T. Gouzadou	KNA Thangkhanla	NPP T. Gouzadou *By-elec.* Thangkhanlian	JD (U) N. Zatawn	MSCP Thangso Baite

had strong grass root base. Not only the elections were fought on ideological differences and political agenda, but also electorates equated themselves with a particular party. Such a phenomenon is not only dwindling but is forcefully taken over by blind support to the highest bidder. Except for small party cadres of Congress, CPI and MPP, no other party seem to enjoy any grass root base. The existing party cadres are insignificant in number to play any decisive role.

Loss of party base started in the mid '80s with new forces of money and muscle powers backing the trend of personal cult then emerging. Regional parties floated in 1990s carry the echo of this personal cult solely on non-constitutional factors. Parties like Manipur State Congress Party (MSCP) and Manipur National Conference (MNC) were formed by the breakaway group from the Congress with no specific political agenda or ideologies. Though most of the regional parties are formed out of breakaway groups of the Congress Party. The differences can be made between regional parties formed before 1990 and the after. Manipur People's Party formed in late '60s still carries specific ideological stand and committed grass root workers. Loss of party base may not be exclusively seen as a case of political bankruptcy. Rather, it may be seen as a compulsion of a small state to go to the tune of political power and alliance at the centre, a perception that had been forcibly fed by the centre from 1973 onwards (Table 1). As mentioned earlier, flourishing of regional party and its government was strongly checked by the Congress government at the centre either by instigating defection or imposing President's rule. Such political vendetta is hard to defend for the less (constitutionally) equipped state government. Survival perhaps is a bigger agenda.

Eighth Legislative Assembly Election 2002

The eighth state Legislative Assembly election held in two phases on February 14 and 21, 2002 was a clear manifestation of the deep-seated disease of political incumbency in the state (Tables 1 and 3). The fact that the seventh state assembly election was held just about two years ago and that the eighth assembly election is preceded by the President's rule only supplement to what was mentioned earlier about the interference of Central government in the affairs of the state. Reasons behind the collapse of MSCP, emergence of Samata Party led rule, and finally President's rule leading to fresh election; are the individual aspirations of MLAs over and above the party values, and dirty hands of power brokers among the Central Leadership (who not only encouraged defection but also instigated one). The fact that MSCP government led by Nipamacha Singh was left to minority barely eleven and half months after being sworn into power shows not only infighting within the party but also backdoor horse trading initiated by the breakaway Congress group in the state and Samata Party at the centre. The rift between the Chief Minister W. Nipamacha Singh's group and Union State Minister Th. Chaoba's faction within the MSCP brought Nipamacha's government into a minority. Added to this were the breakaway 10 Congress and 2 Federal Party MLAs joining Samata Party and with the support of Chaoba faction (and later joined by Nipamacha faction, too) forming the government. The equation took a summersault when in May 2001, 18 MLAs from MSCP joined BJP increasing its strength to 26 that immediately pressed to form the government, which had so far been giving only outside support. Axe finally fell when BJP high command under the pressure from Samata central leadership refused to yield to the pressure of its MLAs to form a BJP led government in the state. Finally the inevitable happened; animated suspension of the House converted into dissolution.

The results of the eighth state assembly election yet again showed signs of lack of direction in which the electorates are. It was a decisive mandate against the former representatives; but expressed more of negative voting than a clear-cut positive mandate. In the light of few major events of defeat and success, the phenomenon reveals a much more complex collective psyche developed consciously or sub-consciously over the last few decades.

The result, mirroring the crises, highlights the following events. One, only 17 members in the 60-member house could stage a comeback (with one not contesting). This accounts for a loss of about 72 percent of the MLAs. Two, it showed that all the political heavyweights, including all the chief ministers except one, failed to retain their seats. Three, though in terms of performance by the political parties distribution of seats in the hills and plains have been evenly shared (Table 5), in terms of political campaigning which was on trans-party line, a divide between two communities — Nagas and Meiteis — was visibly marked out. The attempt was to create ethnic polarisation.

Table 5: Party Positions After the 8th Assembly Election

Parties	Total (60 Seats)		Valley (40 Seats)		Hills (20 Seats)	
	Seats	Votes	Seats	Votes	Seats	Votes
Congress	20	26.2	10	24.8	10	28.3
FPM	13	18.1	10	19.3	3	16.4
MSCP	7	12.4	5	17.3	2	5.1
CPI	5	4.4	5	7.4	0	0.0
BJP	4	9.5	2	5.0	2	16.2
Samata	3	8.3	1	3.0	2	16.3
NCP	3	9.4	2	6.0	1	14.6
Others	5	11.7	5	17.3	0	3.1

Highlights of 72 percent loss of the former MLAs is shown in comparison between the seventh and eighth state assembly elections. That the fast pace of unfolding of events in the last two years brought about a drastic change in the percentage of the success stories of the MLAs. In the seventh state assembly election, 29 MLAs could stage come back. On the contrary, only 17 MLAs could retain their seats in the eighth state assembly. From a 52 percent to 72 percent loss is indeed a big figure considering that the event took place within a span of two years. However, studying few more assembly elections of the past, it showed rather a trend than an exception (Table 6). The only uniqueness in this figure is the issues and time frame under which the entire events unfolded. In the sixth state assembly election only 16 MLAs initially retained their seats, and 2 won back after bye-elections taking the total figure to eighteen. But the landslide fall from a figure of 29 (seventh state assembly) to 17 (eighth state assembly) is what made the event a matter of great political concern.

Table 6: Retention of Seats by the MLAs

Assembly Elections	Year	No. of MLAs retaining seat	% of MLAs retaining seat
2nd State Assembly	1974	22	36.6
3rd State Assembly	1980	17	28.3
4th State Assembly	1985	28	46.6
5th State Assembly	1990	23	38.3
6th State Assembly	1995	18 (16 + 2)	30
7th State Assembly	2000	29	48.3
8th State Assembly	2002	17	28.3

The other major event was the unprecedented defeat of all the political heavyweights. The entire former chief ministers except R.K. Dorendro Singh lost. Such a drastic mandate was never witnessed in the history of electoral politics in the state. Loss of Rishang Keishing, who has so far won all the assembly elections right from the first one (1972), also showed the complexity where a tight-rope-walk pleasing the civil societies and insurgent organizations are of utmost importance. While defeat of Keishing was entirely due to the opposition by NSCN (IM) and Naga civil societies, the case of Radhabinod Koijam was largely marked by unpopularity generated by his administrative and economic measures during his three-months old tenure. Factors governing the defeat of these heavyweights including other MLAs were manifolds showing complexity of the ground reality.

Issues and Verdict: An Analysis

For the eighth state assembly election, three major issues were taken up by almost all the political parties: (i) territorial integrity of Manipur, (ii) acute financial crisis, and (iii) law and order (insurgency and peace) in the state. While the issues of territoriality and peace (involving insurgency) were widely discussed throughout the state, financial crisis and mal-governance were additional issues in the valley.

The question on territorial integrity of the state was an emotive and politically crucial agenda in the state. The events arising out of the extension of cease fire between the NSCN (I-M) and Government of India to Manipur had become a watershed in the recent history of Manipur. It brought out a divide in the politics of the state, between hills and valley on the one hand and within the hills between the Kukis and the Nagas on the other (for the areas claimed as Naga territory has not gone without contest from the Kukis). This issue also expectedly invited involvement of insurgents in the elections. Loss of Rishang Keishing for the first time in his political career is a case in point. The issue on 'territory' (under different perspectives) also played a crucial role in the election in the hills, as tribes belonging to the broad conglomerations of the Nagas and the Kukis expectedly voted on 'ethnic lines'. In the valley, in particular, protecting the territorial integrity of the state turned out to be one of the major issues of political debate. Interestingly, however, there was not a single party left out which could afford to ignore the territorial issue, to plead for Manipur's territorial integrity. In fact, many of the former MLAs (who were attacked by the public) have been projected as torchbearers for the cause of 'territorial integrity'. The new political party, DPP, mainly harped on this agenda.

On the issue of economy, people and leaders were equally aware that no political party could come out with specific measures to tackle the financial crisis, such as irregularity in payment of salaries, financial overdraft, generating state revenues, etc. Yet non-inclusion of the same in the party manifesto could be suicidal. A political party that could come out with sincere and practicable measures might affect voting behaviour on the either side — the fear of backlash. However, with all said, in the backyard of the hype the ceasefire issue carried, the spectacle of politics based on personality, money and muscle power still played its role, and that too with much significance.

This lack of 'direction' as the electoral result showed is largely due to unavailability of proper political space for the exercise of electoral options. While the existing parties and the elected representatives have collectively failed without exception, and there is lack of an alternative, very little is left for the people to make their choices. Thus we see a trend of negative voting in most of the constituencies. Rejecting of former MLAs by the electorates resulting in 72 percent loss of standing MLAs highlights the trend.

The election results send out at least one message clearly — that it was quite obvious as to whom the verdict was against, if not whom it was for. The fact that a positive verdict was not given by the electorates implies at least two possibilities; (i) that people's voice is divided due to differences in perceptions, or (ii) that people are completely disillusioned with the states of affair, their priority areas being diverted and political leadership failing them each time. From the survey conducted by the Centre for the Study of Developing Societies, Delhi,[11] and from the turn of events witnessed in the last few years, the latter showed a stronger reason for providing the kind of fractured mandate that has left the state back geared. Various priority areas like the basic amenities which the citizens ought to get remains unattended, not to talk of fulfilment. Efforts, if made, are meagre and only microscopic. The point for worry is that the fractured mandate has accentuated the already existing deep-rooted political crisis. While no party is in a position to execute its party agenda, all that is witnessed is the willy-nilly of politicking where each party and individual MLAs are engaged in tying and untying the knots of political alliance. In the process, 'governance' gets neglected.

Where loopholes in the anti-defection law are easily found out and MLAs change party loyalty at the slightest pretext, it is but natural to see the governance left unattended. Priority area remained confined only in maintaining political stability. Even after one year of Congress led Secular Progressive Front (SPF) ministry in the office, its foundation looks still shaky. Most of the election time promises are yet to be fulfilled. Meanwhile, several problems have added up. The government is faced with an upheaval task of not only clearing the crises the state had been facing before and at the time of the election, but also the immediate task of containing the ever-disgruntled ministers and MLAs who are still threatening to change sides in the wake of any shift in the balance of power. The recent phenomenon (April 2003) had been the displeasure shown by some ministers against the chief minister's stringent financial directives, which could in a spurt of moment lead to the downfall of the ministry. Little lessons seem to have been learnt from the past experience.

Lack of governance has led the creation of several socio-political crises getting magnified into giant size macro-level issues. A crisis unattended in its initial stage has generated further crisis, thus leading to multiplication of one over another. A two-fold problem arises: on the one hand political leadership fails to contain the macro level crises, on the other the basic programmes of governance remain unattended. In turn, an explosive circle is created. The state gets engaged only at the task of fire fighting where basic issues are almost forgotten. The present state of affair of which election result was one such manifestation shows the level of crisis the state and its people are presently faced with. The solution lies in political stability. This can be maintained only with a new legislation that will strongly check horse-trading and frequent shift of party loyalty.

NOTES AND REFERENCES

1. However, recent trend has been that the so-called 'national parties' are also becoming 'regional' in outlook where discourse of politics is the state. In short, an exclusive dichotomy between regional and national parties is fast changing. A new way, perhaps a third category, has to be found out to study the new trend. This does not however mean that the distinctness of the two outlooks is erased. The differentiation is still conditionally valid.
2. Sanamahi is the pre-Vaisnava religion followed by the Meiteis. It also refers to the Meitei god under whose name the religion came to be known. Still a good number of Meiteis follow the Sanamahi religion. Meitei Hindus (including the Brahmins), too, worship Sanamahi, the Meitei God.
3. The term Mayangs refers to the mainland Indians comprising of Punjabi, Marwari, Bengali, Tamil, etc.
4. *Fact File*, All Manipur College Teachers' Association, 2001.
5. Recently, there had been instances in the district of Tamenglaong, inhabited by Zeliangrong Nagas, where minority non-Christians were being physically targeted and abused by the majority Christians. This of course has not been in large scale. One may as well take note of Meitei-Pangal clash where the divide was on the basis of Meiteis and Manipuri Muslims.
6. New names/categories of communities like Naga, Kuki or Zeliangrong are political constructs based on ethnic closeness of the tribes falling under this category. The term 'ethno-political' is preferred over 'political'.
7. Except for tribes like Anal, Maring and Moyon who are classified as New Naga/Old Kuki, ethnically falling in the Kuki-Chin group but preferring to be called Naga in the new political formation, the division and exclusivity between Nagas and Kukis, politically, is widening.
8. Pattern of 'temporarily homogenising' otherwise scattered population has been discussed by Christophe Jafferlot in detail in case of Babri-Masjid conflict. See, Christophe Jafferlot, 'The Politics of Procession and Hindu-Muslim Riots', in Amrita Basu and Atul Kohli (eds.), *Community Conflicts and the State in India*, Oxford University Press, New Delhi, 1998.
9. The latest crisis in a different form is the ongoing debate on clearing the proposed plan of Tipaimukh dam project. Five Naga organizations, viz. United Naga Council, Naga Women's Association, Committee against Tipaimukh Dam, Naga People's Movement for Human Rights, and all Naga Students' Association (all from Manipur), have registered strong protest not merely by way of debate but by going for popular protests. What is noteworthy is that the dam is to be constructed at Churachandpur district mainly inhabited by Hmars, Paite and Thadous, whereas more likely affected areas are in Tamenglong mainly inhabited by the Zeliangrong Nagas. Though proposals for construction of two dams in Tamenglong district is already approved without opposition, Tipaimukh dam proposal is facing stiff resistance from the Naga civil societies with the argument that number of displaced people will be around 40,000. This goes against the Government's survey report of estimated 1000 affected villagers after the proposed height of the dam was reduced by 10 metres. The intensified movement started in October 2002 and is continuing till date.
10. Kuki's claim for Sadar Hills district as a full-fledged revenue district is based on British creation of Sadar sub-division in 1933 with its headquarter at

Kangpokpi. Nayal Commission (1974) recommended inclusion of few villages of Senapati and Ukhrul districts into the proposed district. The proposal was for better administrative convenience and development. Nagas have opposed the inclusion of any Naga villages in the proposed district.

11. CSDS's Lokniti conducted a survey on the voting behaviour of the electorates during the assembly election in Manipur from 14 to 18 February 2002 and has come out with some informative data. The survey was conducted in twelve constituencies, eight in the valley and four in the hills, in the ratio of 2:1, considering the fact that there are in total, out of sixty, forty constituencies in the valley and twenty in the hills. The method of selection was based on 'probability-proportionate-to-size.' We also made it sure that proportionate distribution is made between Naga and Kuki dominated areas among the hill constituencies. Two polling stations from each constituency were selected through 'random sampling'. The sample of respondents was randomly drawn from the electoral rolls of the selected booths. There were in total 646 respondents interviewed. Twenty-eight volunteers from different colleges at Imphal participated at the survey work. Infrastructural support was provided by Taibang Paojen, the newspaper group based at Imphal. For further details, see, Bhagat Oinam, 'Manipur Assembly Election: Manifestation of Growing Crises', *Economic and Political Weekly*, 6–12 July 2002.

APPENDIX-I

Demographic Profile of the Five States in the Region

State	Population			Percentage decadal growth		Literacy rate		
	Persons	Male	Female	1981–91	1991–01	Persons	Male	Female
Assam	26,638,407	13,787,799	12,850,608	24.24	18.85	64.28	71.93	56.03
Nagaland	1,988,636	1,041,686	946,950	56.08	64.41	67.11	71.77	61.92
Manipur	2,388,634	1,207,338	1,181,296	29.29	30.02	68.87	77.87	59.70
Meghalaya	2,306,069	1,167,840	1,138,229	32.86	29.94	63.31	66.14	60.41
Tripura	3,191,168	1,636,138	1,555,030	34.30	15.74	73.66	81.47	65.41

Source: Provisional Census Data 2001.

APPENDIX-II

Electorate in Constituencies of Respective States

State		Gen (40 seats)	SC (1 seat)	ST (19 seats)	Total (60 seats)
Manipur	Male	431383	9865	277264	718512
	Female	464280	10173	279917	754370
	Total	895663	20038	557181	1472882
State		Gen (102 seats)	SC (8 seats)	ST (16 seats)	Total (126 seats)
Assam	Male	6004654	520610	985228	7510492
	Female	5515172	486980	926523	6928675
	Total	11519826	1007590	1911751	14439167
State		Gen (5 seats)	SC	ST (55 seats)	Total (60 seats)
Meghalaya	Male	NA	NA	NA	6,44,913
	Female	NA	NA	NA	6,34,827
	Total	NA	NA	NA	1,279,740
State		Gen (1 seat)	SC	ST (59 seats)	Total (60 seats)
Nagaland	Male	NA	NA	NA	527,583
	Female	NA	NA	NA	486,216
	Total	NA	NA	NA	1,013,799
State		Gen (34 seats)	SC (6 seats)	ST (20 seats)	Total (60 seats)
Tripura	Male	5,90,749	1,00,893	3,10,510	10,02,152
	Female	5,47,049	91,416	2,94,526	9,32,991
	Total	11,37,798	1,92,309	6,05,036	19,35,143

Source: Calculated from data of States' Election Commissions and Election Commission of India.

APPENDIX-III

Votes Share of Major Political Parties during the Last Three Assembly Elections

Assam	Parties	1991	Parties	1996	Parties	2001
	BJP	6055	BJP	8.39	BJP	9.35
	INC	29.32	INC	30.10	INC	39.75
	JD	4077	ASDC	1.98	NCP	20.02
	Left parties (CPI & CPM)	6.31	Left parties (CPI & CPM)	3.84	Left parties (CPI & CPM)	2.88
	AGP		AGP	29.55	AGP	20.02
	NAGP		URMCA	—	URMCA	0.16
	ASDC	1.59	AIIC (T)	2.42	ASDC (U)	1.11
	URC	1.31	—	—	ASDC (P)	0.92
	IND	21.39	IND	12.40	IND	19.51
Meghalaya	**Parties**	**1993**	**Parties**	**1998**	**Parties**	**2003**
	INC	34.62	INC	35.03		
	BJP	3.68	BJP	5.01		
	HPU	21.53	UDP	26.99		
	APHLC	7.93	GNC	2.11		
	HSPDP	9.80	HSPDP	6.77		
	PDM	2.14	PDM	6.95		
	MPP	2.47	—	—		
	IND	17.28	IND	16.16		
Manipur	**Parties**	**1995**	**Parties**	**2000**	**Parties**	**2002**
	INC	28.65	INC	18.31	INC	26.18
	BJP	3.35	BJP	11.28	BJP	9.55
	CPI	5.59	CPI	3.60	CPI	4.40
	JD	11.92	JD (U)	1.79	—	—
	SAP	6.19	SAP	6.68	SAP	8.33
	ICS	3.91	JD (S)	1.58	MNC	4.03
	MPP	23.67	NCP	7.87	NCP	9.44
Meghalaya	**Parties**	**1993**	**Parties**	**1998**	**Parties**	**2003**
	FPM	4.91	MMP	7.90	MMP	3.03
	—	—	MSCP	26.28	MSCP	12.40
	—	—	FPM	9.44	FPM	18.14
	—	—	—	—	DRPP	3.93
	IND	7.73	IND	3.01	IND	0.33

Tripura	Parties	1993	Parties	1998	Parties	2003
	INC	32.73	INC	33.96	Congress & INPT	45.00
	BJP	2.02	BJP	5.87	BJP	0.45
	CPI	1.35	CPI	1.38	Left Front (CPI, CPM & RSP)	51–19
	CPM	44.78	CPM	45.49	—	—
	—	—	JD	0.24	—	—
	RSP	1.58	RSP	1.65	—	—
	TUJS	7.52	TUJS	7.19	—	—
	AMB	1.46	AMB	0.32	NA	NA
	JD (B)	1.57	—	—	NA	NA
	IND	6.16	IND	3.29	NA	NA

Nagaland	Parties	1993	Parties	1998	Parties	2003
	INC	46.02	INC	50.73	INC	35.85
	BJP	0.35	IND	49.27	BJP	10.87
	NPC	32.82	—	—	NCP	1.99
	DLP	0.51	—	—	NDM	9.52
	IND	20.29	—	—	NPF	29.77
					JD (U)	5.80
					SAP	1.76
					AITC	0.33

Source: Calculated from data of States' Election Commissions and Election Commission of India.

APPENDIX-IV

Contesting Parties in Respective States

State	National Parties	Recognised States Parties	Unrecognised States Parties
Assam	Indian National Congress (INC) Bharatiya Janatà Party (BJP) Communist Party of India (CPI) Communist Party of India (Marxist)	All India Trinamool Congress (AITC) Communist Party of India (Marxist-Leninist) (Liberation) CPI (ML)(L) Assam Gana Parishad (AGP) Samajwadi Party (SP) Samata Party (SAP) Rastriya Janata Dal (RJD) Rastriya Lok Dal (RLD)	Natun Assam Gana Parishad (NAGP) Autonomous State Demand Committee (ASDC) Barak Valley Territory Demand Committee (BVTDC) Janata Party (JP) United Bodo Nationalist Liberation Front (UBNLF) United Minorities Front of Assam (UMFA) United Reservation Movement Council of Assam (URMCA) United Peoples Party of Assam (UPPA) Hindusthan Suraksa Party People's Democratic Front Plains Tribals Council of Assam Trinamool Gana Parishad United People's Party of Assam United Tribal Nationalist liberation Front

State	National Parties	Recognised States Parties	Unrecognised States Parties
Meghalaya	Indian National Congress (INC) Bharatiya Janata Party (BJP) Nationalist Congress Party (NCP) Communist Party of India (CPI)	Hill State People's Democratic Party (HSPDP) Peoples' Democratic Movement (PDM) United Democratic Party (UDP) Samajwadi Party (SP) Rastriya Janata Dal (RJD) Samata Party (SAP)	All Party Hill Leaders Conference (Armison Marak Group) Khun Hynniewtrep National Awakening Movement (KHNAM) Meghalaya Democratic Party (MDP) Garo National Council (GNC) Khasi Farmers Democratic Party
Manipur	Indian National Congress (INC) Bharatiya Janata Party (BJP) Nationalist Congress Party (NCP) Communist Party of India (CPI)	Samajwadi Party (SP) Samata Party (SAP) Janata Dal (United) Federal Party of Manipur (FPM) Manipur Peoples Party (MPP) Manipur State Congress Party (MSCP)	Manipur National Conference (MNC) Manipur Peoples Party (Democratic) Democratic Revolutionary Peoples Party Kuki National Assembly Naga National Party National Peoples Party
Nagaland	Indian National Congress (INC) Bharatiya Janata Party (BJP) Nationalist Congress Party (NCP)	Samata Party (SAP) Janata Dal (United) All India Trinamool Congress Rastriya Lok Dal (RLD)	Nagaland Democratic Party (NLDP) Nagaland Peoples Front (NPF) Nationalist Democratic Movement (NDM)
Tripura	Indian National Congress (INC) Bharatiya Janata Party (BJP)	Revolutionary Socialist Party (RSP) Indigenous Nationalist Party of Twipra (INPT) All India Trinamool Congress (AITC)	All India Forward Bloc (AIFB) Amra Bangalee (AMB)

Bibliography

Abbi, B.L. (ed.), *North East Region: Problem and Prospects of Development*, Centre for Research in Rural and Industrial Development, Chandigarh, 1984.

Barpujari, H.K. (ed.), *Political History* of Assam, Vol. 1, Government of Assam, Gauhati 1977.

Baruah, A.K. "Nationalism, Regionalism and the Problem of Integration" in *In Search of India's Rennaisance*, Vol. II, Centre for Research in Rural and Industrial Development, Chandigarh, 1992.

Baruah, A.K. and Goswami, Sandhya, "Fractured Identities: Politics in a Multi-Ethnic state", *Economic and Political Weekly*. August 21–28, 1999.

Baruah, A.K. and Kumar, Pramod, "Why Do Voters Not Vote?' *Economic and Political Weekly*, Vol. Nos. 51–52.

Baruah, A.K., "Mainstream Political Science and its Pit Falls" *Proceedings of the North East India Political Science Association*, Second Annual Conference, Guwahati, 1992.

Baruah, A.K., *Social Tension in Assam: Middle Class Politics*, Purbanchal Prakash, Gauhati; 1990.

Baruah, A.K., "Reorganization of Composite Assam and the Linguistic Chauvinism of the Asomiyas", *Proceedings of the North East India history Association*, Seventeenth Session, *Aizawl*, 1997.

Baruah, Apurba K. (ed.), *Student Power In North East India*, Regency, New Delhi, 2002.

Baruah, Apurba K., "Tribal Traditions And Crises of Governance In North East India With Special Reference To Meghalaya" *Crisis States Working Papers*, Working Paper No. 22 (www.crisisstates.com).

Baruah, Nirode K., *David Scott in North-East India, 1802–1831: A Study in British Paternalism*, Munshiram Manoharlal, New Delhi, 1969.

Basu, Amrita and Kohli, Atul (eds.), *Community Conflicts and the State in India*, Oxford University Press, New Delhi, 1998.

Bedrock of Naga Society Published by NPCC-I. Kohima, 2000.

Bose, Ashish *et al.* (ed.), *Tribal Develpoment and Demography in North-East India*, B.R. Publishing, Delhi, 1990.

Burdick, E. and Brodbeck, A. (eds.), *American Voting Behaviour*, Free Press, Glencoe, 1959.

Campbell, A., Gurin, G. and Miller, W.E., *The Voter Decides*, Row Peterson, Evanston, 1954.

Chaube, S.K., *Electoral Politics In North East India*, Sangam Books, London, 1985.

Dastur, Aloo *et al.*, *Voting Pattern in Bombay*, Bombay, University, Bombay, 1967.

De, Ranjit Kumar, *Socio-Political Movements in India*. Mittal Publications. N. Delhi. 1998.

Deka, K.M. *et al.*, *Election Politics in Assam*, Bani Prakashan, Guwahati, 1987. Delhi, 1994.

Election Commission of India — State Election, 1969 to the Legislative Assembly of Nagaland.

Election Commission of India — State Election, 1974 to the Legislative Assembly of Nagaland.

Election Commission of India — State Election, 1977 to the Legislative Assembly of Tripura.

Election Commission of India — State Election, 1987 to the Legislative Assembly of Nagaland.

Election Commission of India — State Election, 1998 to the Legislative Assembly of Nagaland. February 15–21, 2003.

Frankel, Francine *et al.*, *Transforming India*, Oxford University Press, New Delhi, 2000.

Gogekar, S.V. and Richard Park (ed.), *Report on the Indian General Elections: 1951–52*, Popular Book Depot, Bombay, 1956.

Guha, Amalendu, *Planter Raj To Swaraj*, ICHR. N. Delhi, 1977.

Gupta, Sushmita Sen, Communist Party of India in Meghalaya, unpublished M.Phil. thesis, North Eastern Hill University, Shillong, 1988.

Hansaria, B.L., *Sixth Schedule to the Constitution of India — A Study*, Gita Hansaria, *Gauhati*, 1983.

Hazarika, Sanjay, *Strangers of the Mist*. Penguin Books India Ltd: N. Delhi. 1994. http://www.eci.gov.in http://www.nenanews.com

Kothari, Rajni, "The Take Off Election", *Economic Weekly*, July 1962.

Lazersfeld, P.F., Berelson B. and Gaudet H., *The People's Choice: How the Voter Makes up his Mind in a Presidential Campaign*, Columbia University, New York, 1944.

Lok Sabha General Elections 1984. Detail Election Results, Chief Electoral Officer, Kohima Nagaland.

Luthra, L.N., *Nagaland from a District to a State*. DIPR. Arunachal Pradesh, Shillong, 1974.

Macpherson, C.B., *The Real World of Democracy*, Oxford University Press, New York, 1972.

Merriam, C.E. and Gosnel, H.F. *Non-voting: Causes and Methods of Control*, University of Chicago, Chicago, 1924.

Misra, Udayan, *The Periphery Strikes Back: Challenges to the Nation-State in Assam & Nagaland*. IIAS: Shimla, 2000.

Misra, Udayan, "Naga Peace Talks: High Hopes and Hard Realities." *Economic & Political Weekly*.

Misra, Udayon, *North East India: Quest for Identity* (Omsons Publications). Delhi, 1988.

Mitra, Subrata, *Culture & Rationality*, Sage India, N. Delhi.

Moriss Jones, W.H., " The Indian Elections" *Economic and Political Weekly*, June 28 and July 5.

Mukherjee D.P., "First Fruits of General Elections", *Economic Weekly*, Jan. 26, 1952

Narain, Iqbal, "Political Behaviour in Rural India: the Case of Panchayat Elections in Rajsthan", *Journal of Commonwealth Studies*, July, 1967.

Narain, Iqbal, Pandey, K.C. and Sharma, Mohanlal (Mrs.) Hansa Rajplal, *Election Studies in India: An Evaluation*, Allied, New Delhi, 1978.

Nibedon, Nirmal, *Nagaland — The Night of the Guerrillas*. Lancer. N. Delhi, 2000 reprint. Vol. Nos. 51–52.

Oinam, Bhagat, 'Manipur Assembly Election: Manifestation of Growing Crises', *Economic and Political Weekly*, 6–12 July 2002.

Phukan, Girin, Yasin Adil-ul- (eds.), *Working of Parliamentary Democracy and Electoral Politics in Northeast India* (South Asian Publishers) New Delhi, 1998.

Rekha, Chowdhary and Nagendra Rao, "Elections 2002: Implications for Politics of Separatism". *Economic & Political Weekly*. January 4–10, 2003.

Report on the Eleventh General Elections to the Lok Sabha, 1996 from the Nagaland Parliamentary.

Report on the Tenth General Election to the House of the People from the Nagaland Parliamentary.

Roy Ramashray and Wallace Paul (eds.), *Indian Politics and the 1998 Election*, Sage, New Delhi, 1999.

Roy, Ramashray, *The Uncertain Verdict: A Study of the 1969 Elections on Four Indian States*, Orient Longman, Delhi, 1972.

Sangma, Milton S (ed.), *Essays on North East India*, Indus, New Delhi, 1994.

Sarkar, Jayanta and Ray B. Datta, *Social and Political Institutions of the Hill People of North East India*, Anthropological Survey of India, Calcutta, 1990.

Shadap-Sen, Cathrine Namita, *The Origin and Early History of the Khasi-Synteng People*, Firma KLM, Calcutta, 1981.

Sharma, Manorama, *Social & Economic Change in Assam: Middle Class Hegemony*. Ajanta Publications, N. Delhi, 1990.

Sirsikar, V.M., "The Study of Voting Behaviour in India: Limitations and Problems" *Political Science Review*, May, 1962.

Srivastava, G.L., *Indian Elections and Election Petitions*, Eastern Book Company, Lucknow, 1961.

Statistical Report on General Elections 1964 to the Nagaland Legislative Assembly. http://www.eci.gov.in

Teer, F. and Spence, J.D., *Political Opinion Polls*, Hutchinson, London, 1973.

Verma *et al.*, *Voting Behaviour in a Changing Society: A Case Study of the Fourth General Elections in Rajasthan*, National, Delhi, 1973.

Williams, P., 'Electoral Studies and the 1980 Election in the United States', *Electoral Studies*, 1:

News Papers

Eastern Mirror, Kohima.
Hindustan Times, North East Special.
Nagaland Page, Kohima.
Nagaland Post, Dimapur.
Northeast Herald, Kohima.
The Implanter, Kohima.
The Shillong Times, Shillong.
The Assam Tribune, Guwahati.
The Sentinel, Guwahati.
Asomiya Pratidin, Guwahati.
Aji Daily, Guwahati.
Budhbar, Guwahati.
Sadin, Guwahati.
Natun Samay, Guwahati.

Index